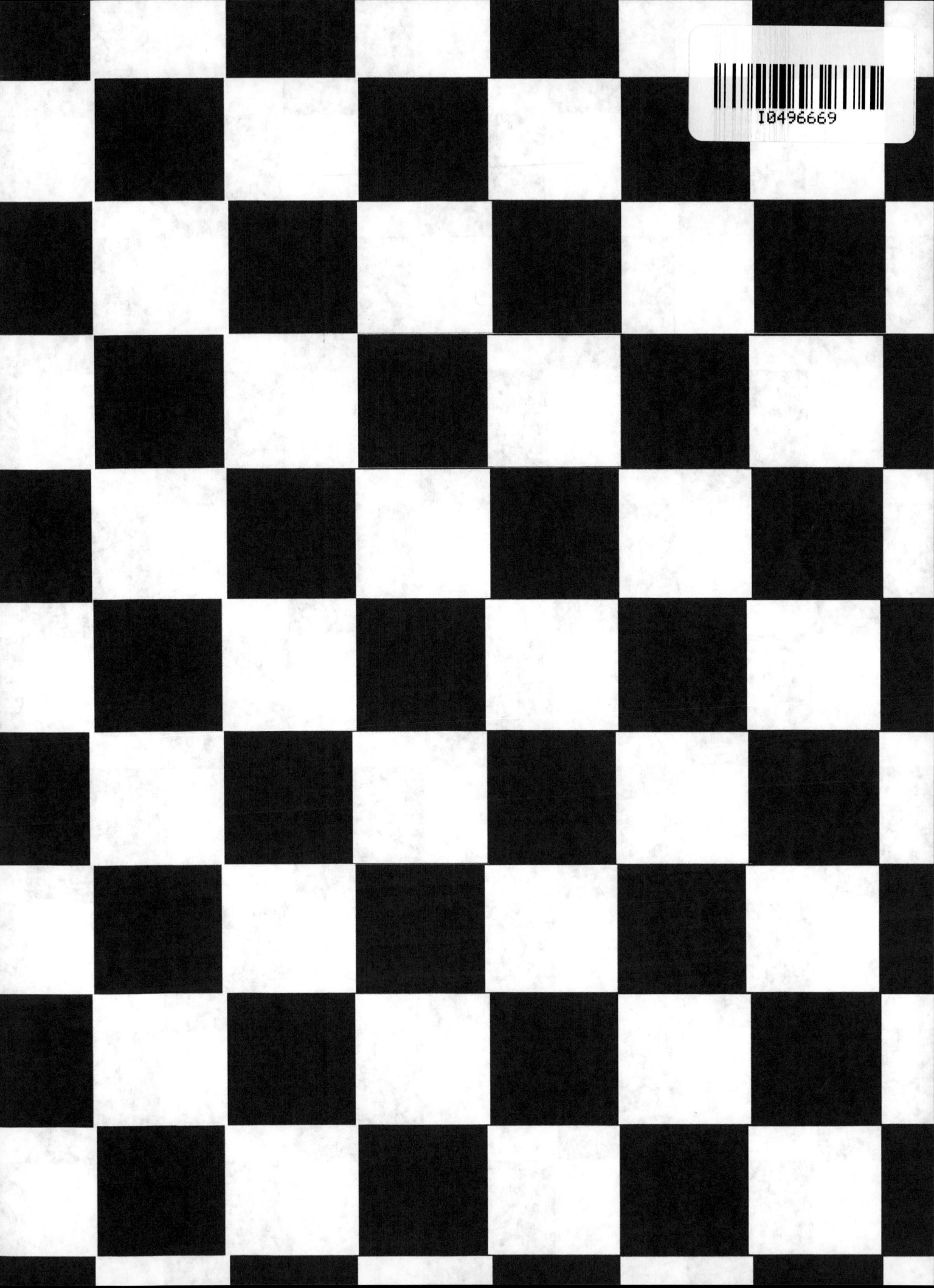

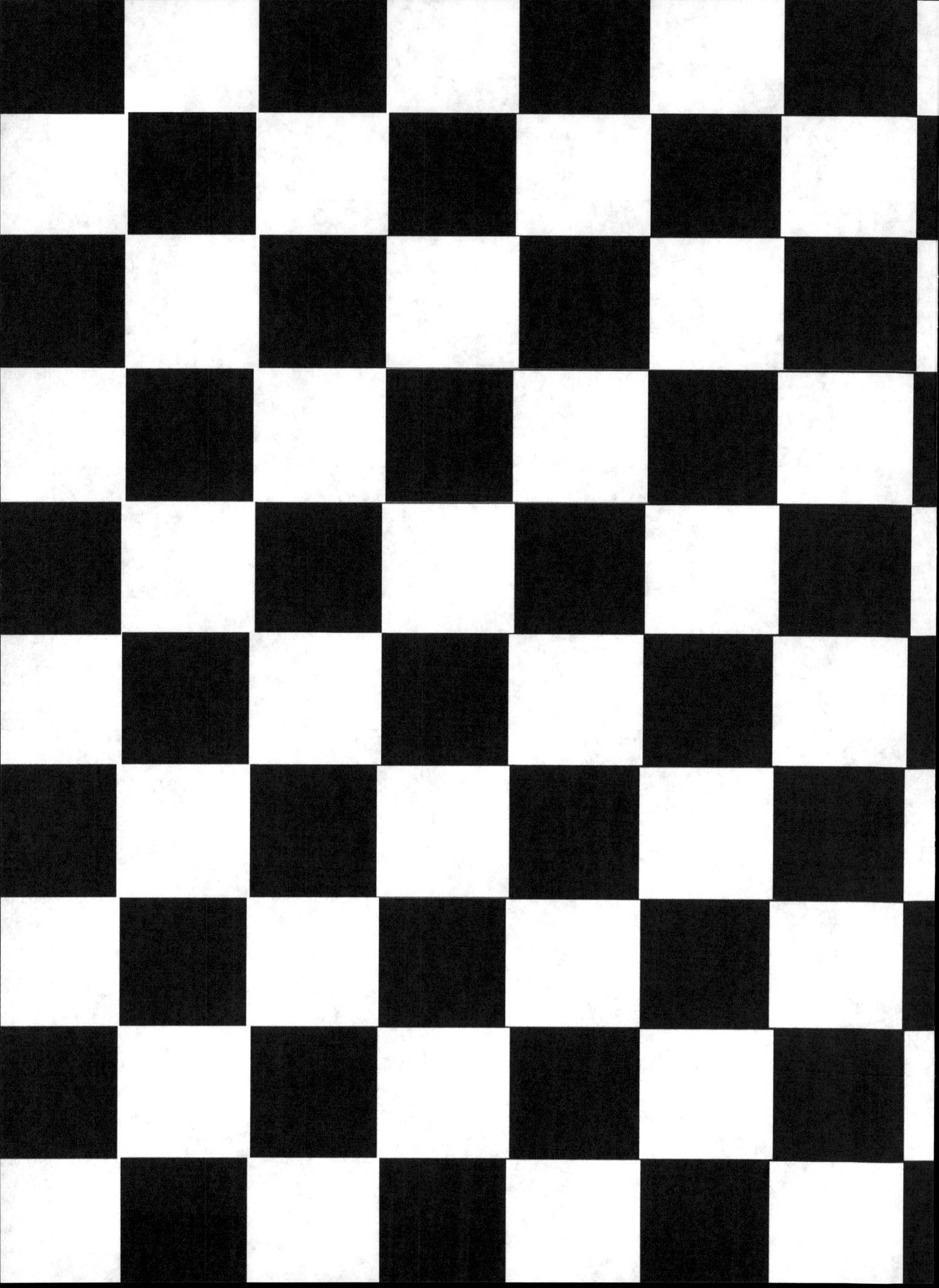

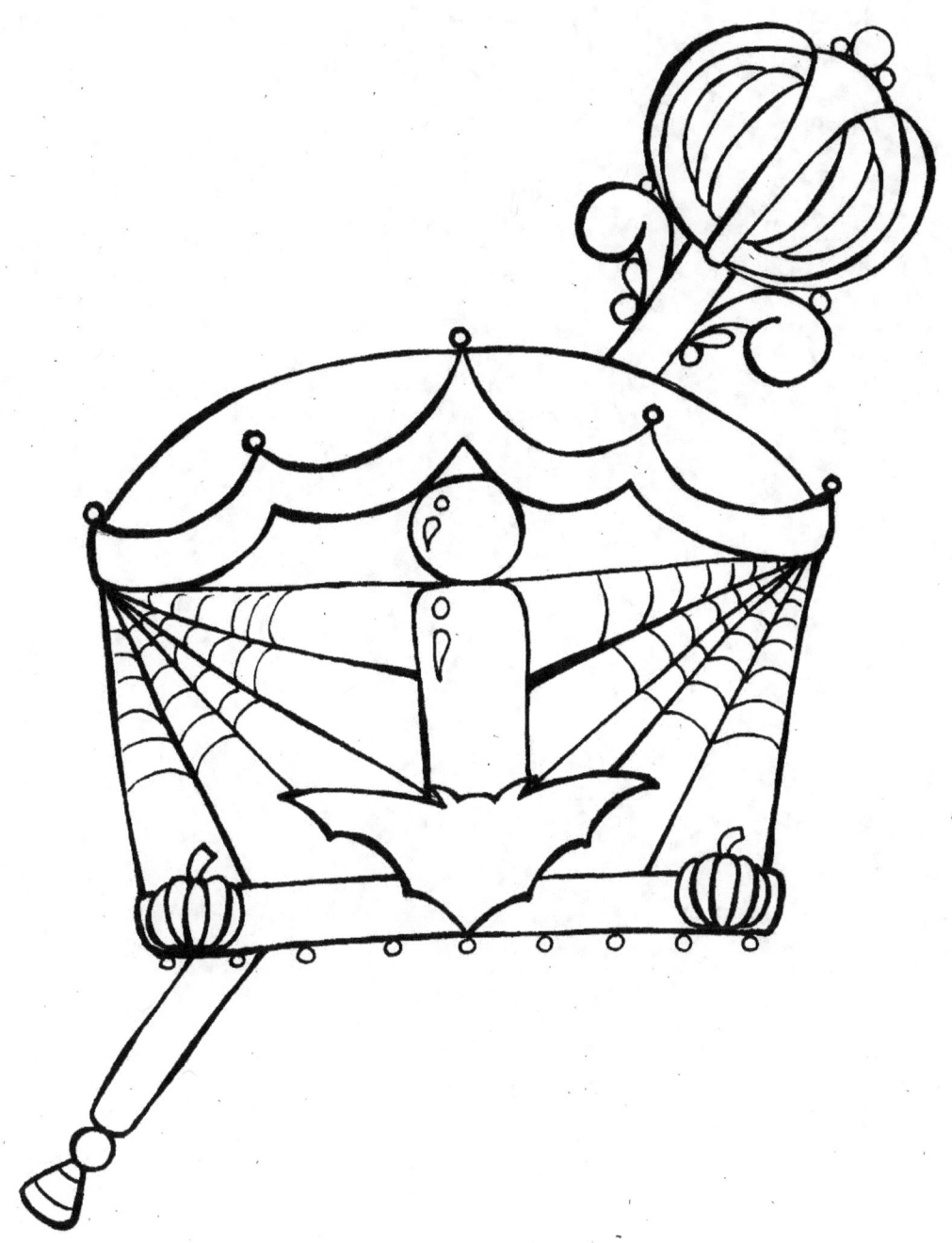

In the world of the Saturnalia, many kingdoms thrive...Including the kingdom of Magia. Magia is a majestic kingdom where the magic of Halloween is everyday life for its Royal Family and its citizens. Legend has it that centuries ago, when civilization as we know it, was in its early stages the king and queen of Magia visited Earth, and lived amongst humans as Gypsies. They offered stories and teachings about the Celebration of Life, an annual month-long festival in Magia where all Magians celebrate and pay tribute to the lives of those whose souls have moved on. King Magicus and Queen Vera rule a super magical, vibrant, and productive Kingdom with their 15 children. Not only does the Royal family of Magia serve as rulers of the land, but they also serve as the protectors of its people. They are the only inhabitants of this kingdom that were born with the special powers it takes to fend of the jealous evil the lives on Saturnalia's large moon, Tritus.

This Coloring Book features 17 portraits of the Royal Family of Magia. Get Creative and bring this Magical Family to life!

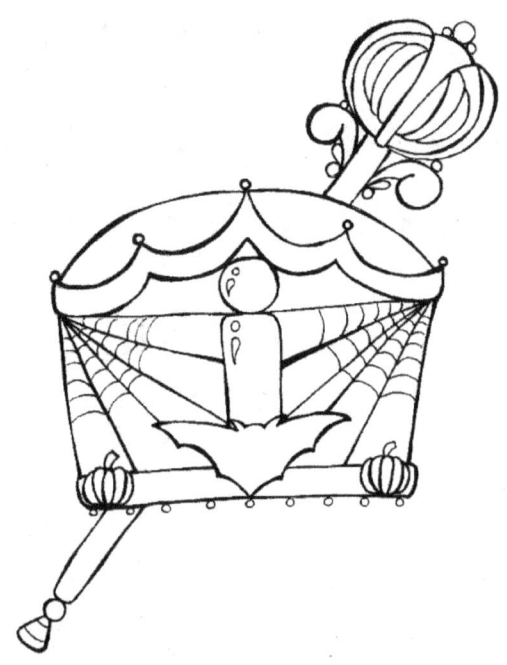

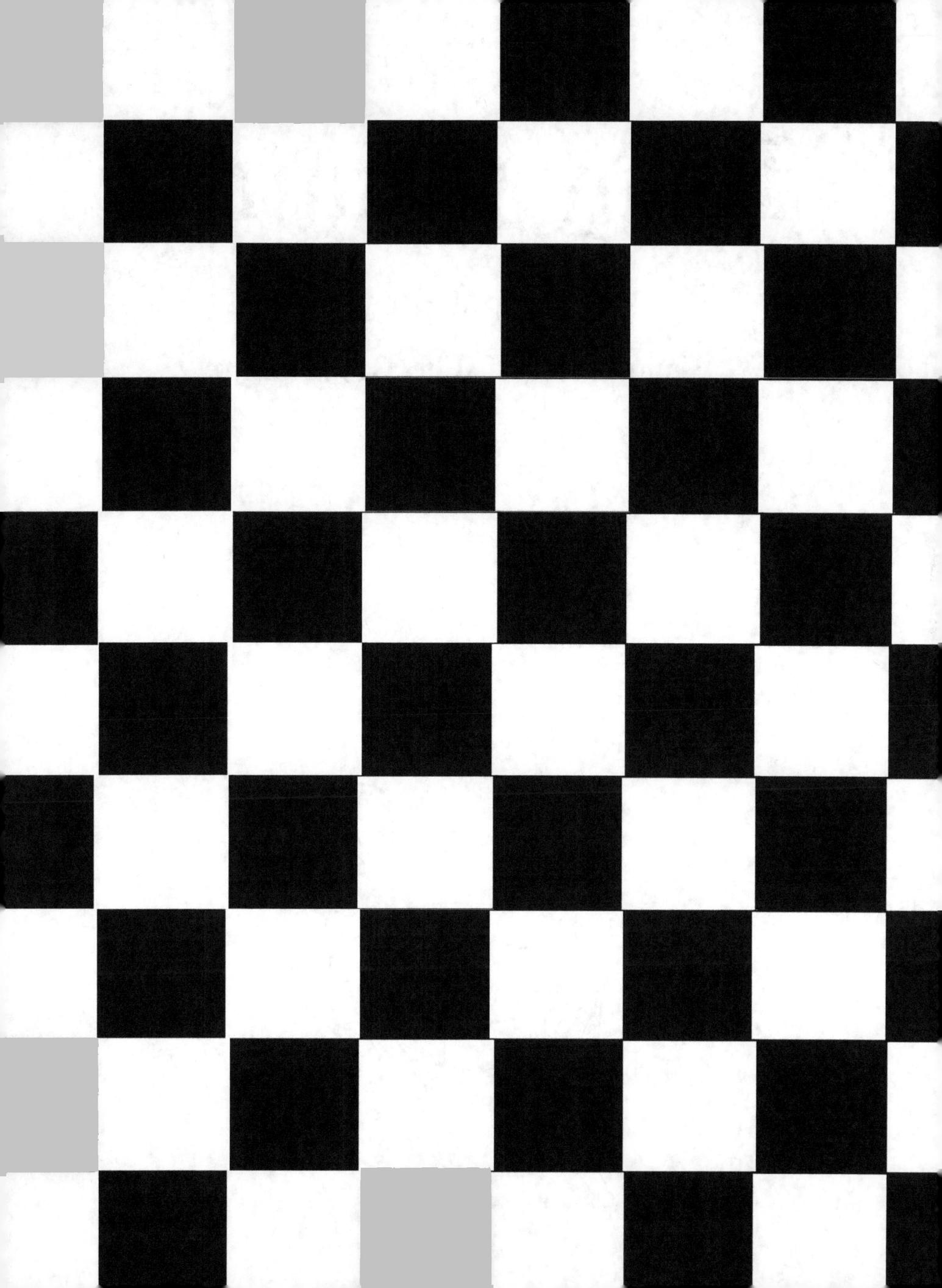

King Magicus

Ruler of Magia
Commander of The Royal Army

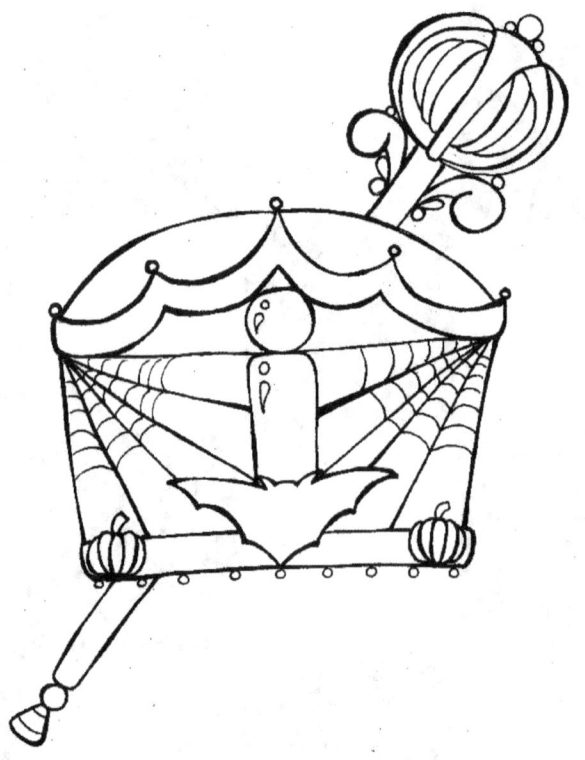

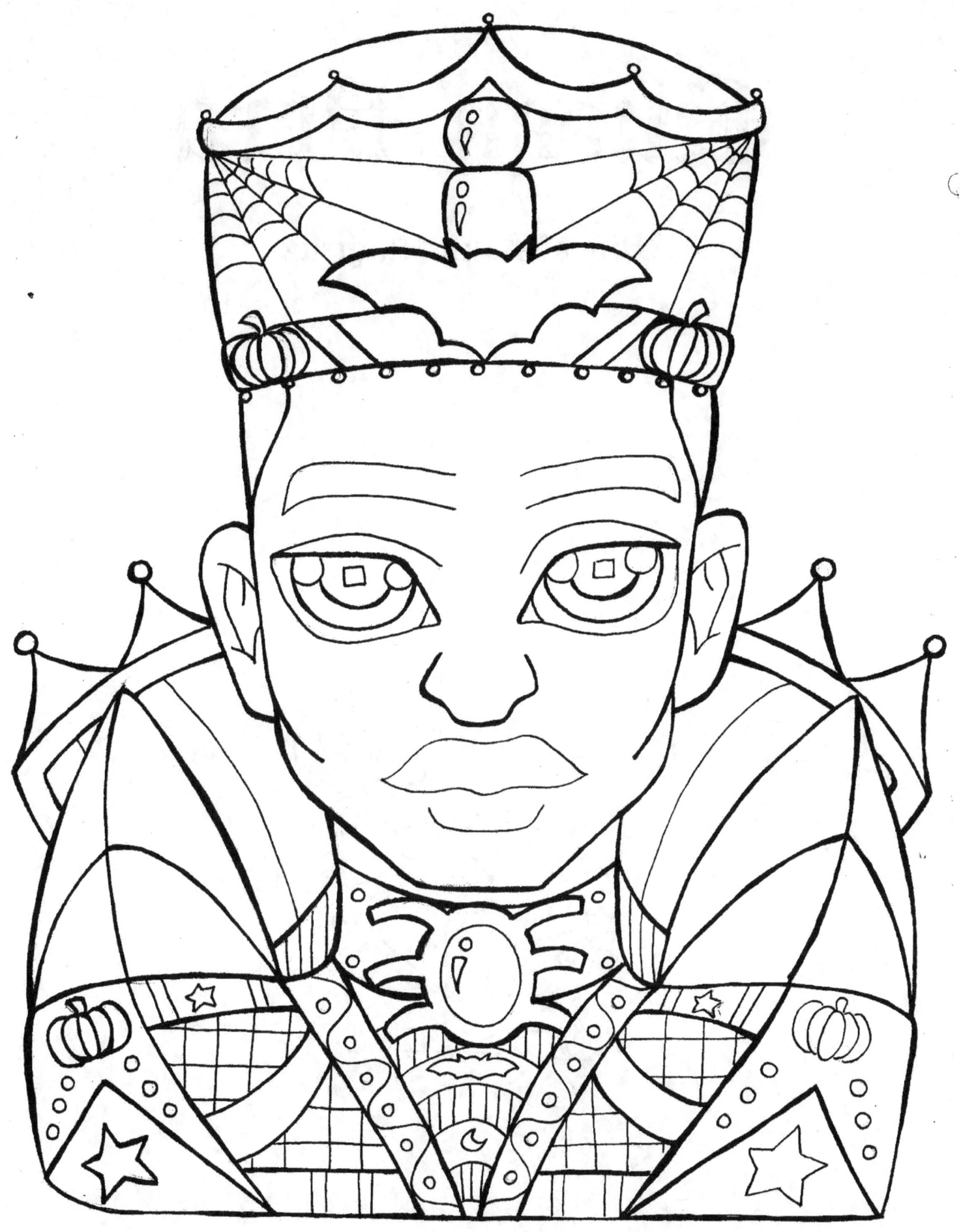

Queen Vera

Wife of King Magicus

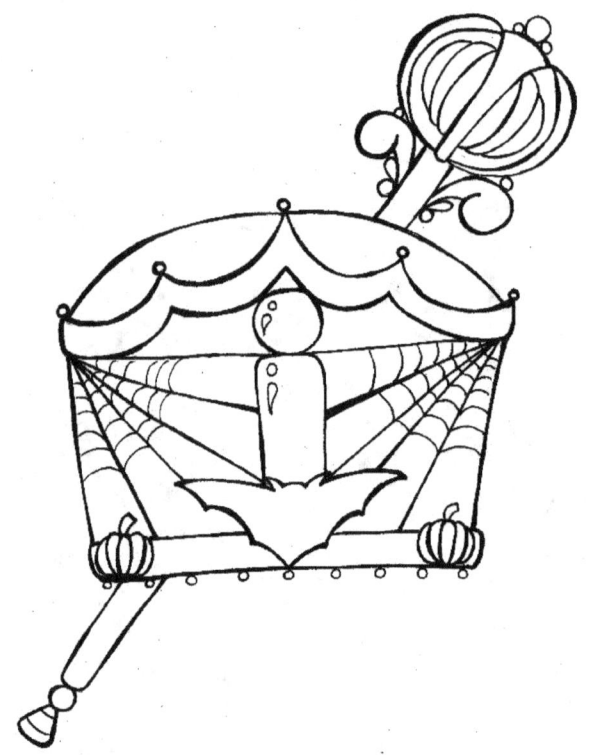

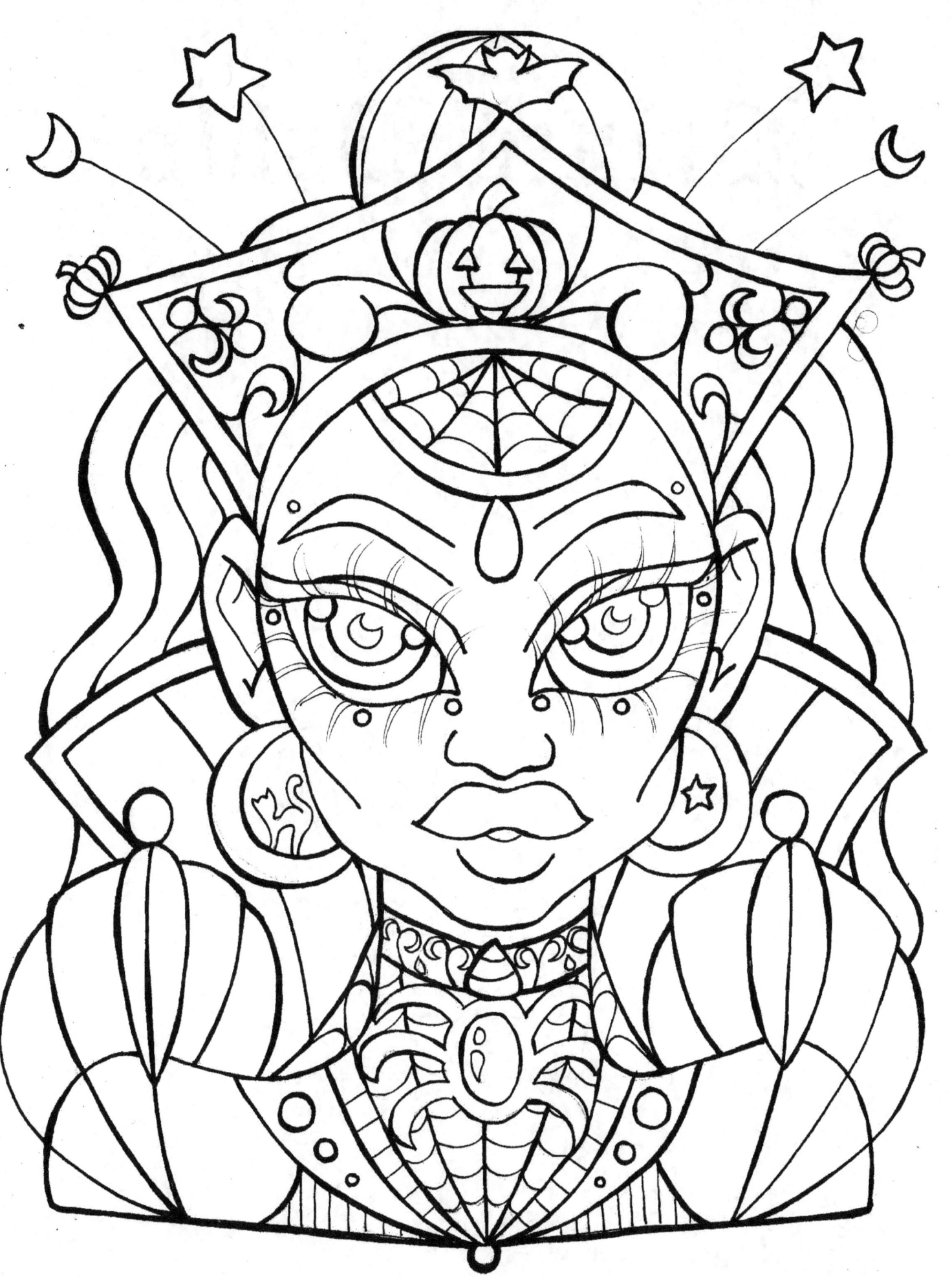

Prince Pablo

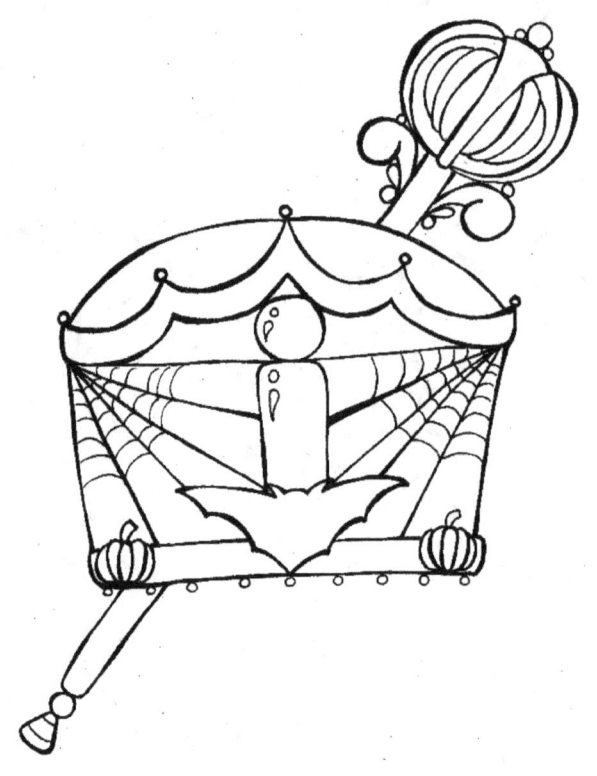

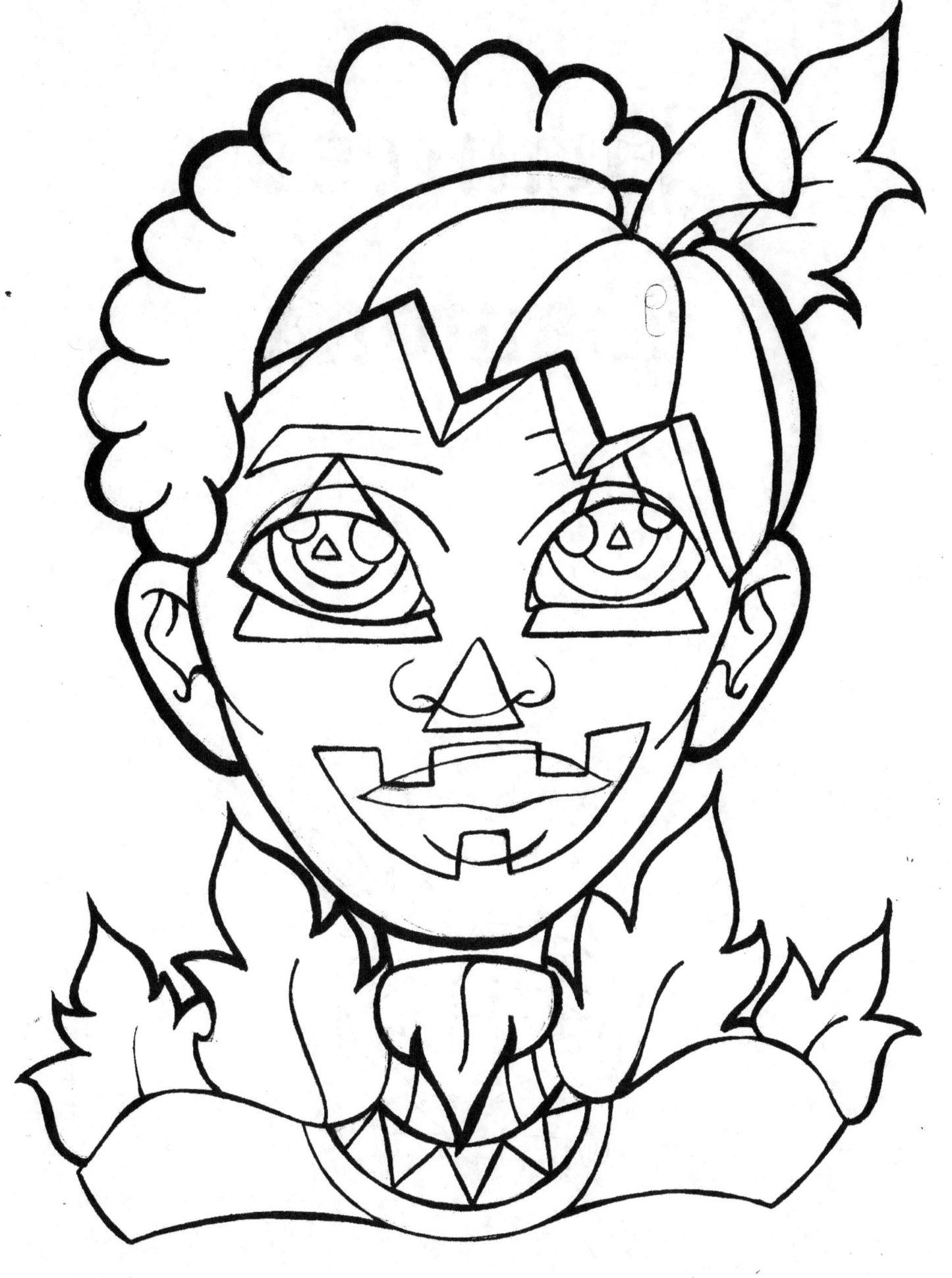

Princess Pamona

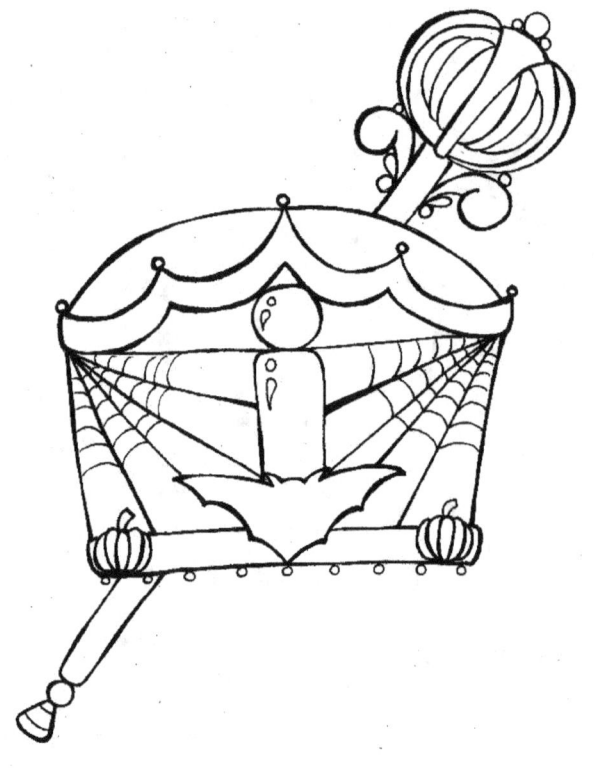

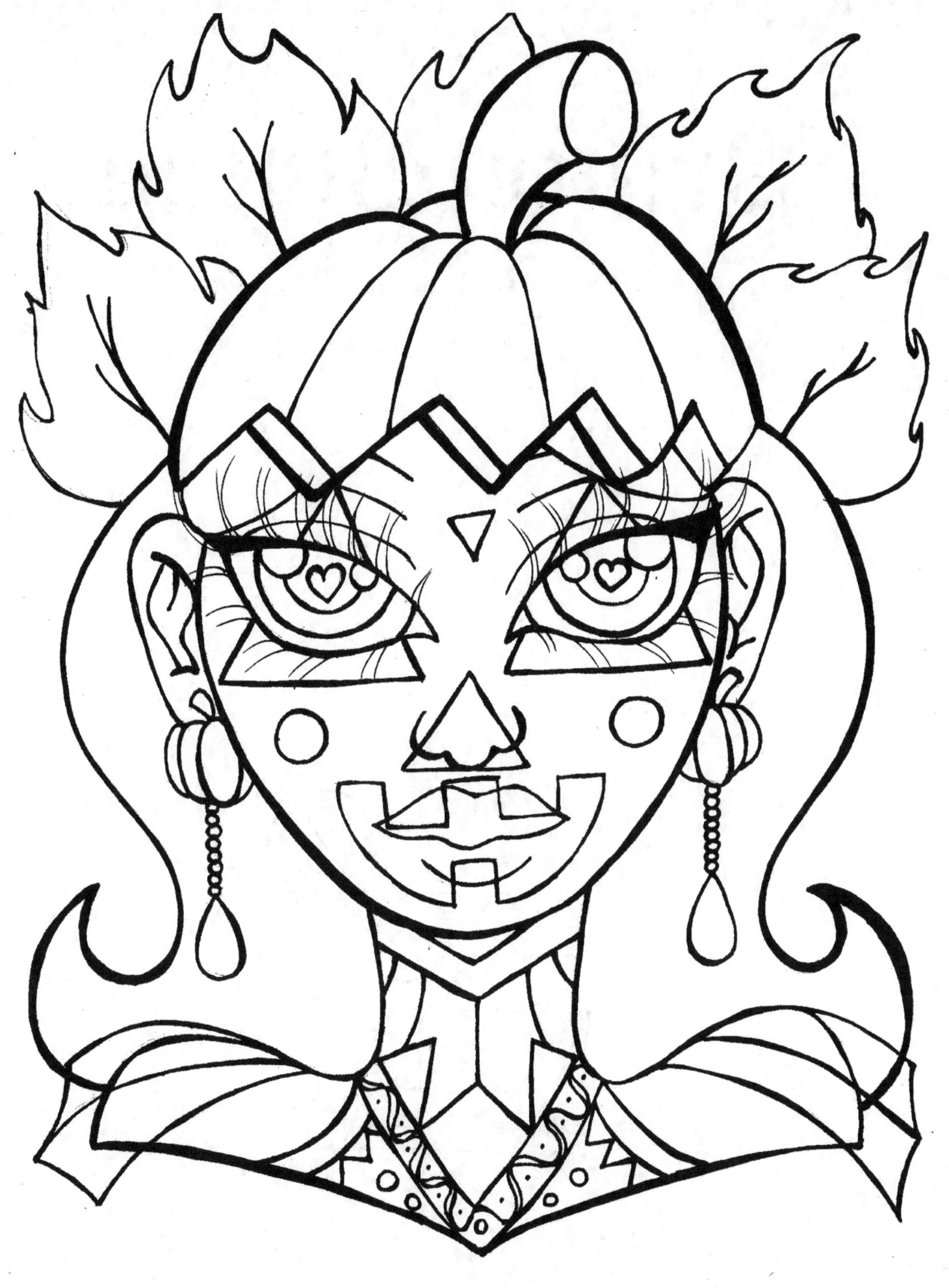

Prince Divino

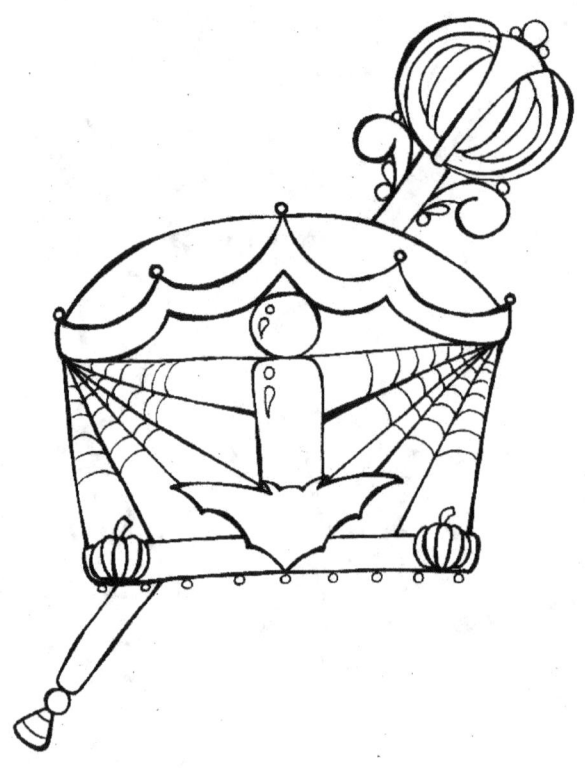

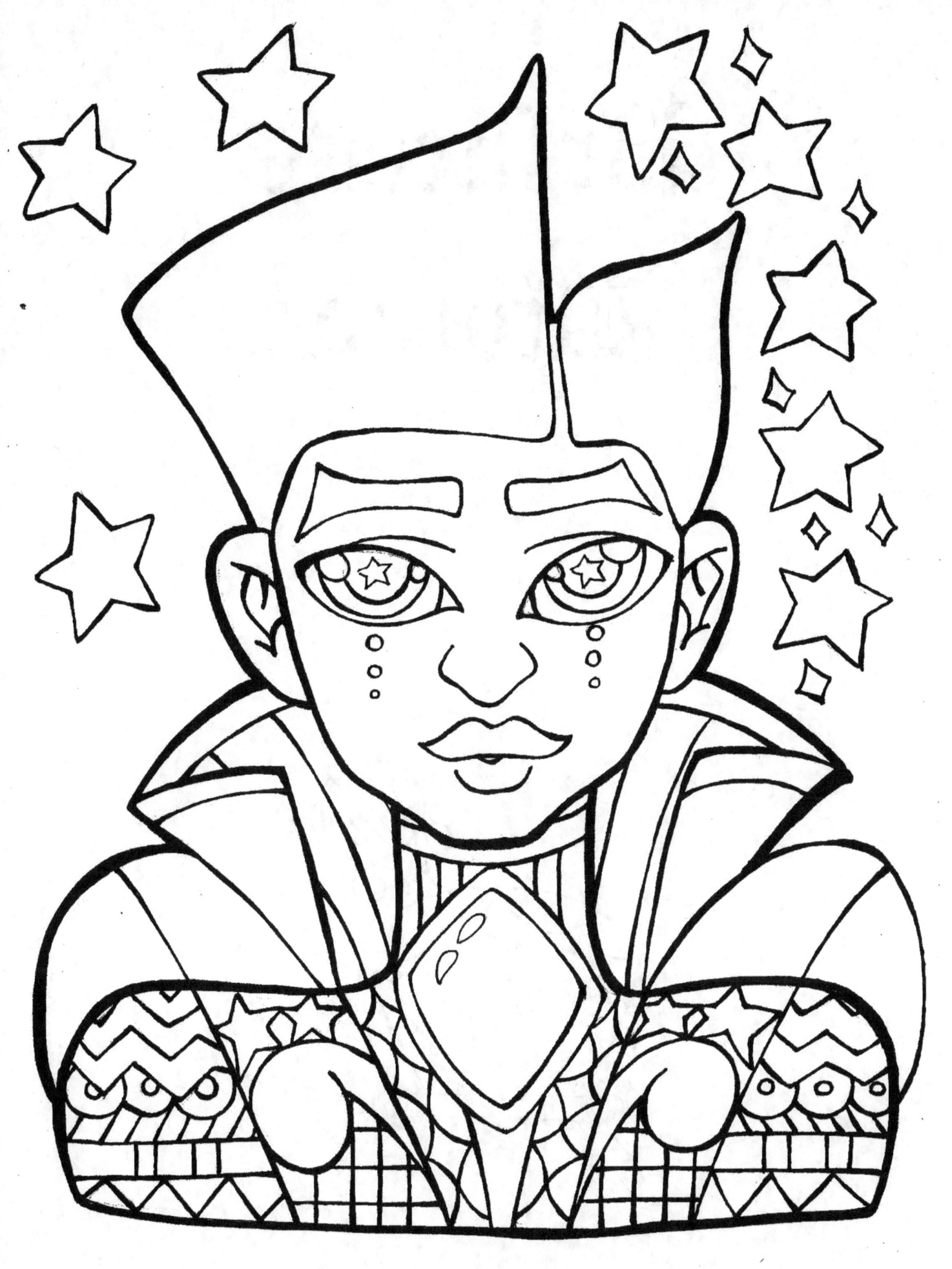

Princess Divina

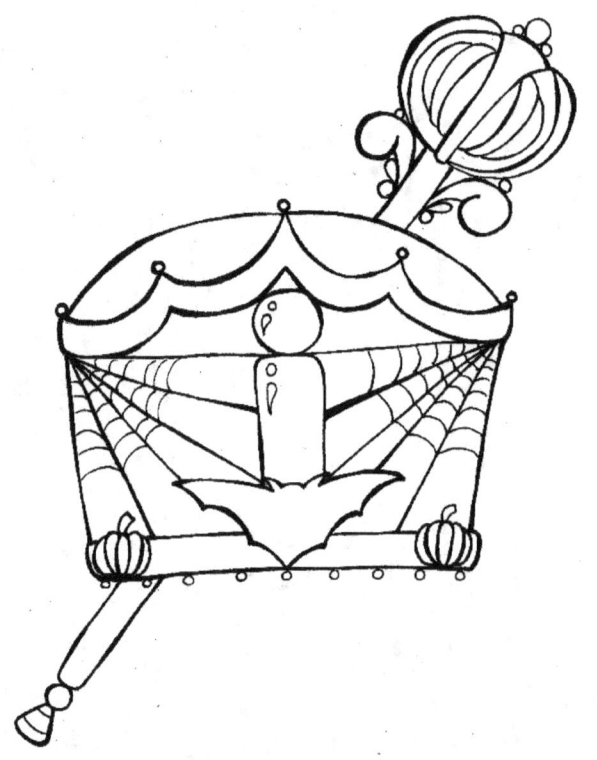

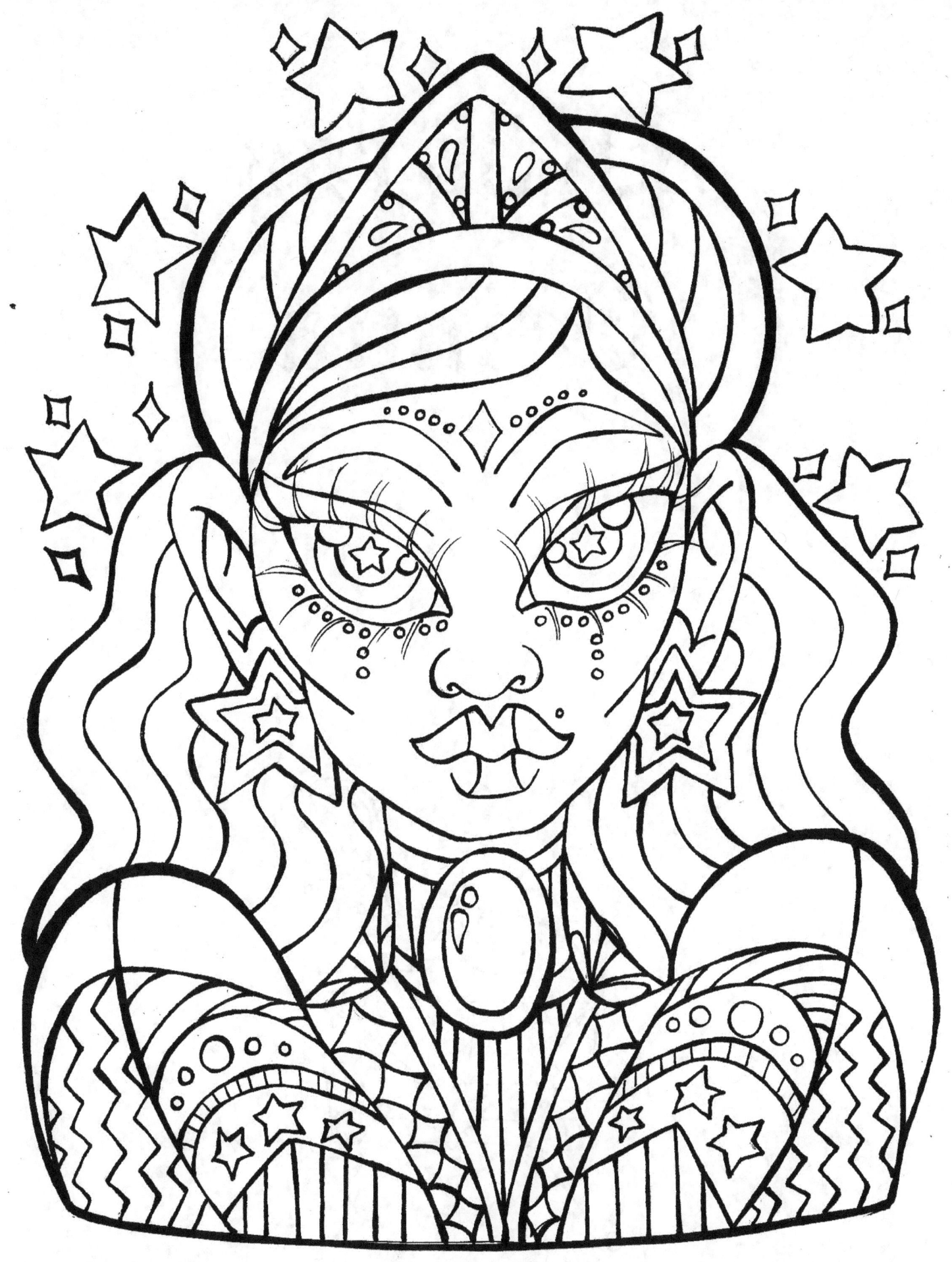

Princess Trinica

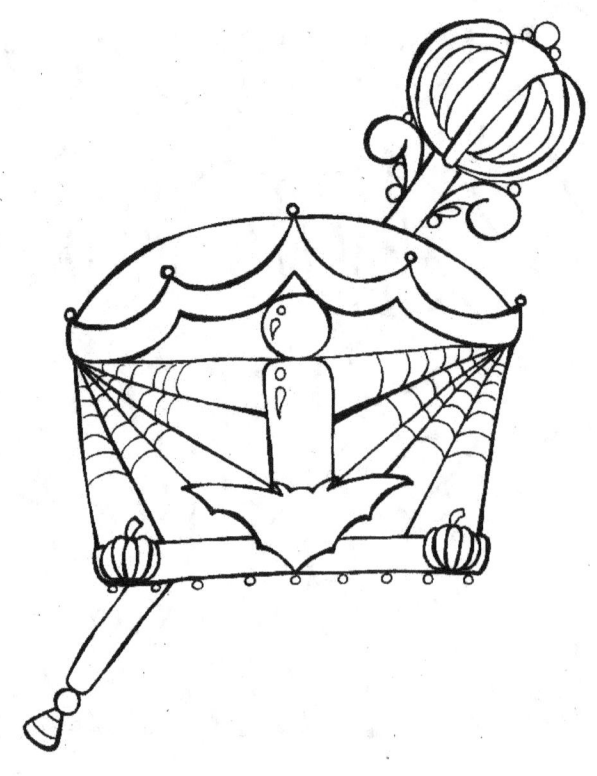

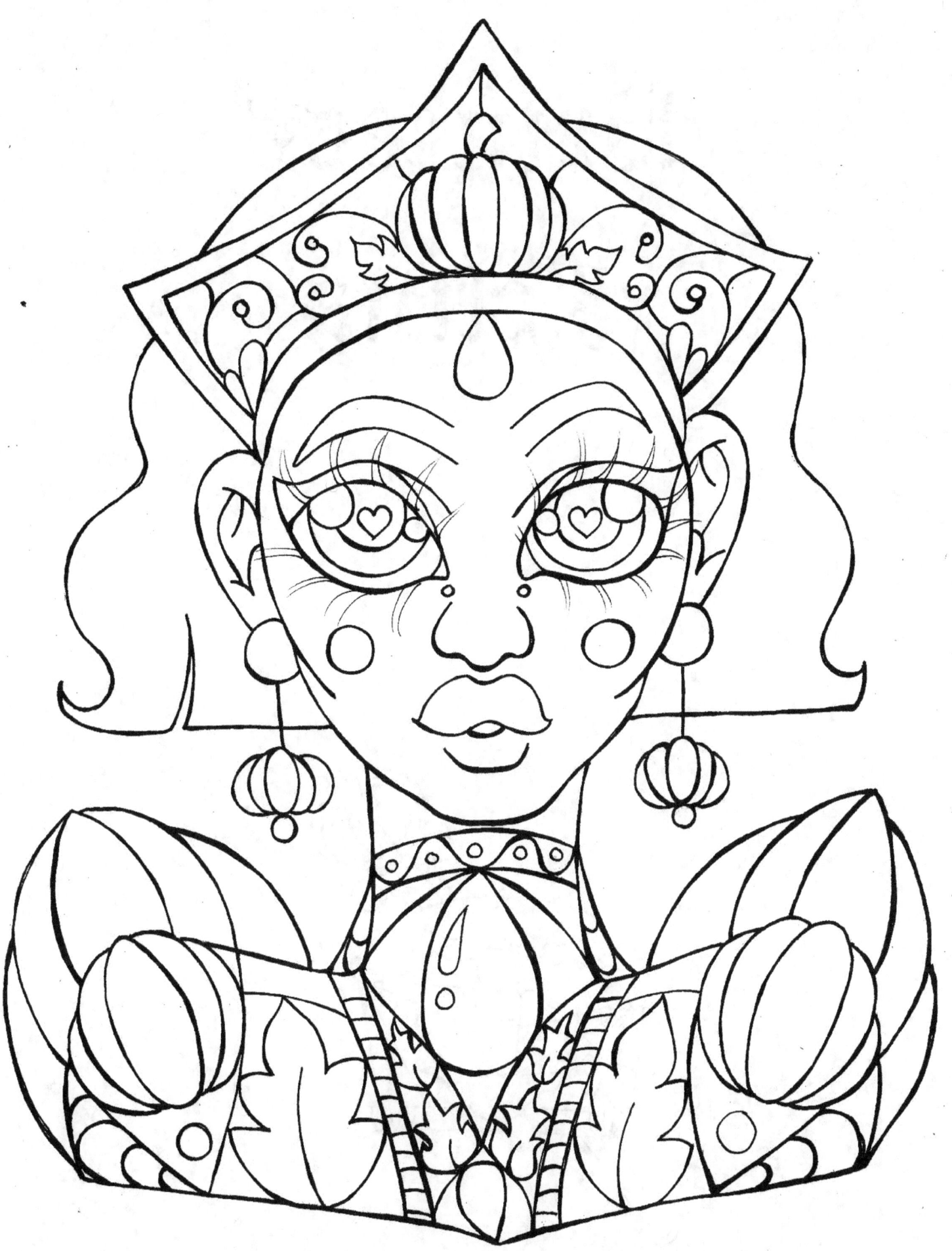

Princess Felina

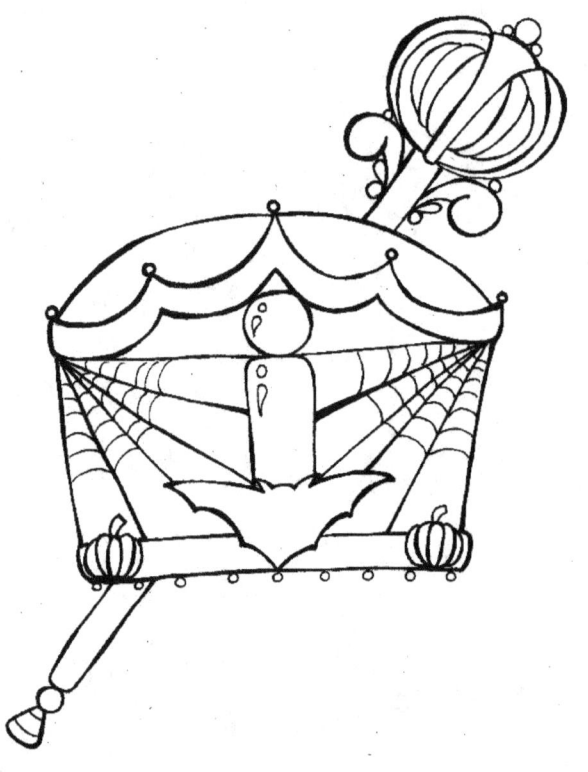

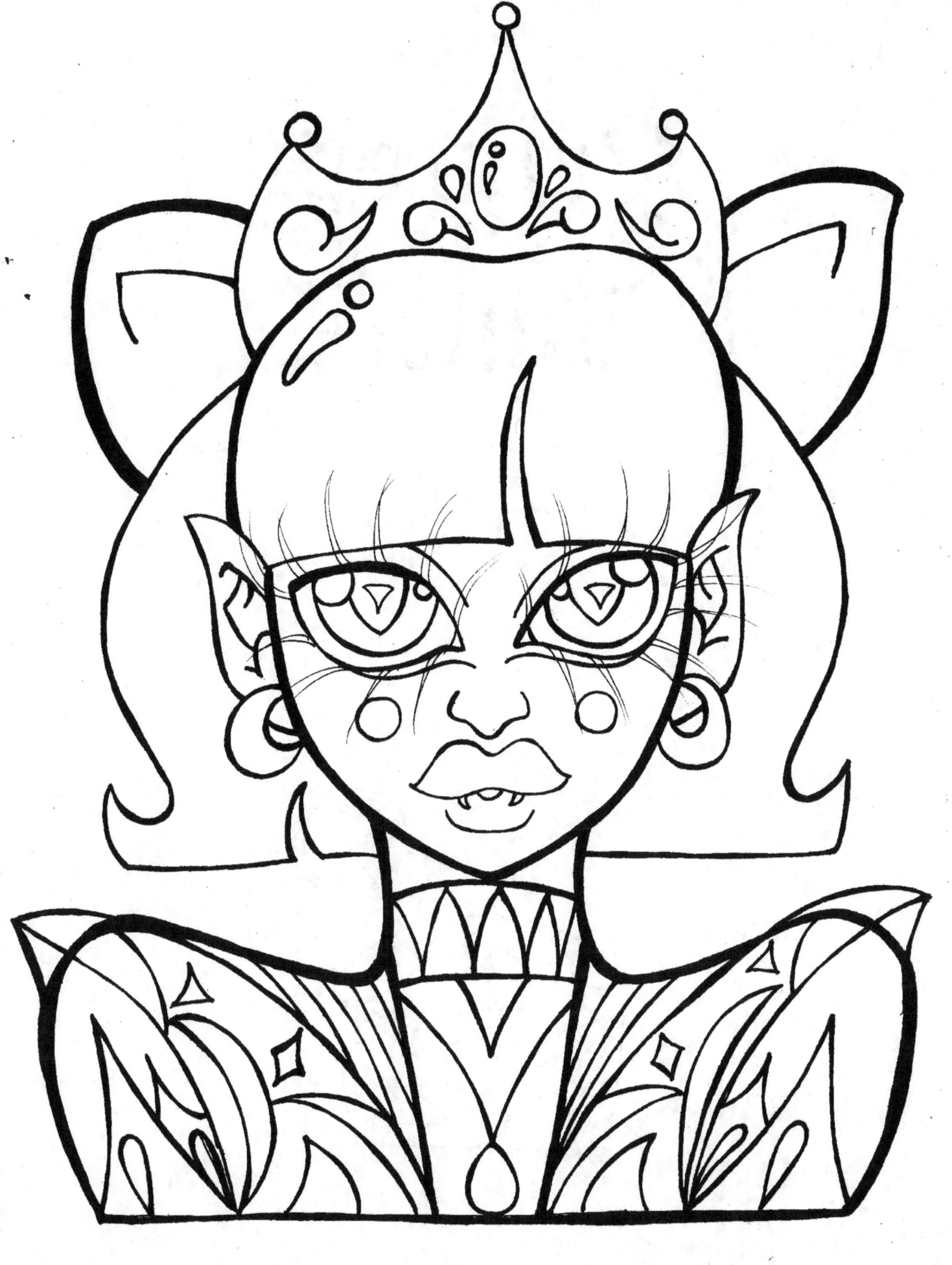

Princess Dulcia

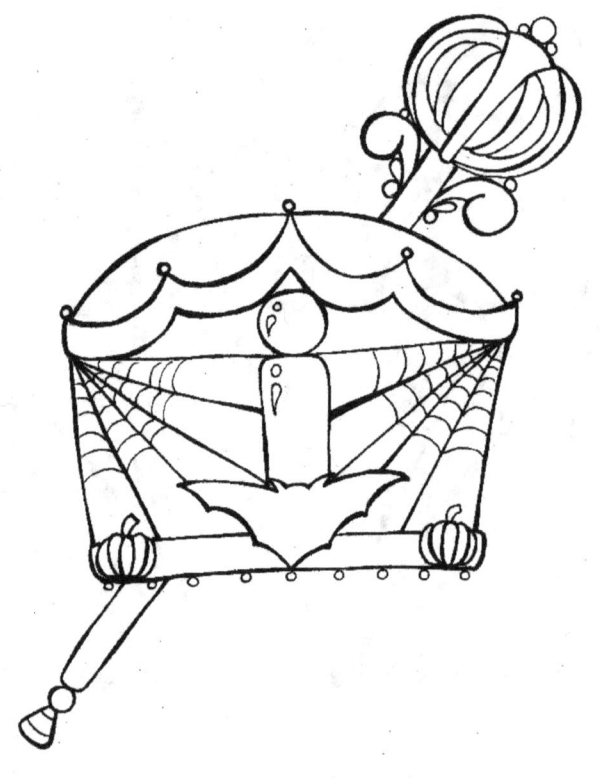

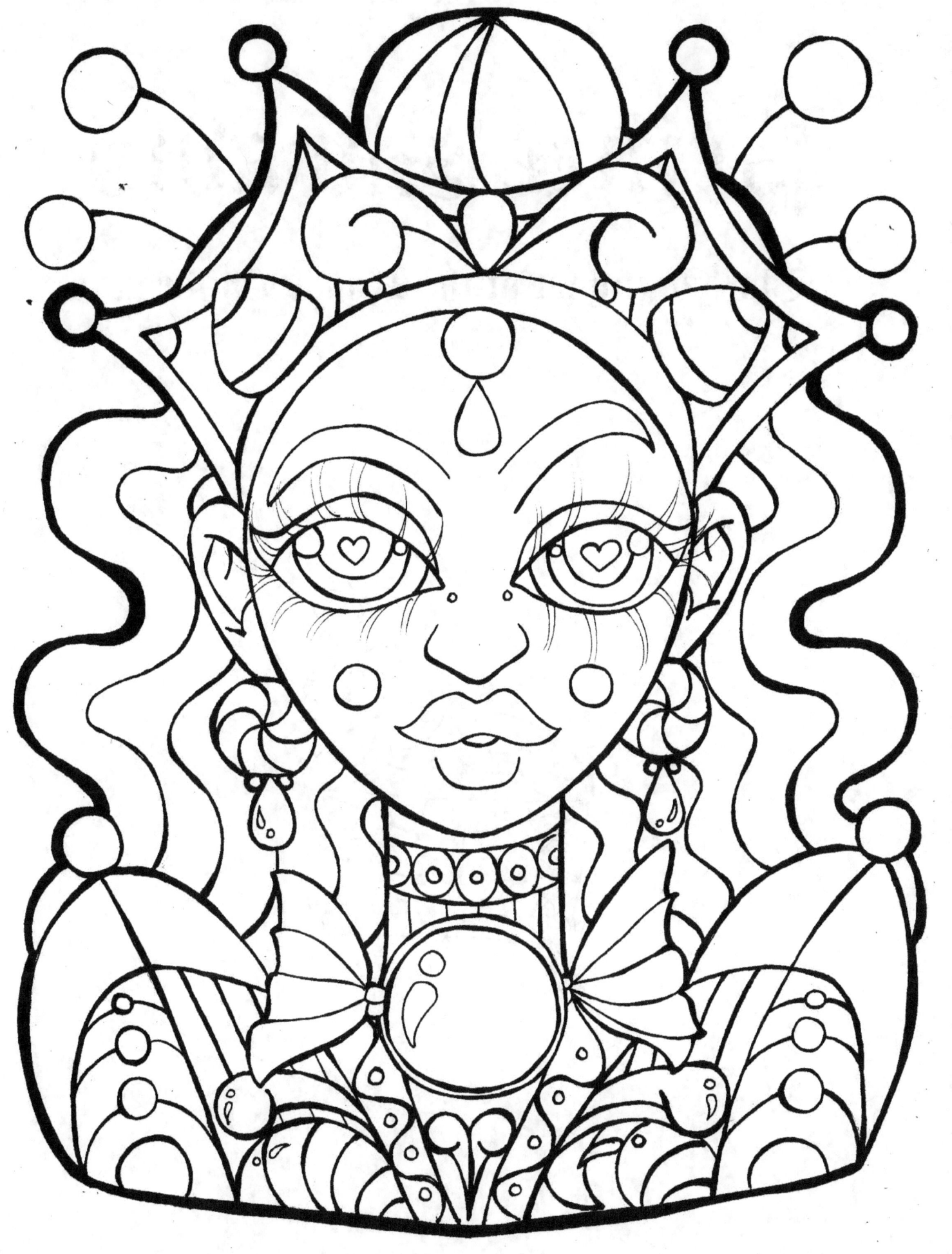

Prince Swavio

The Youngest of the Royal Children

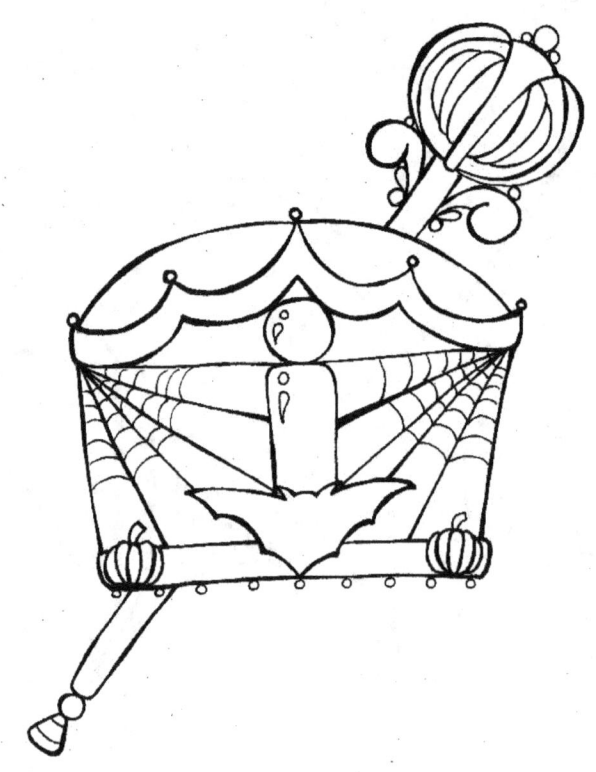

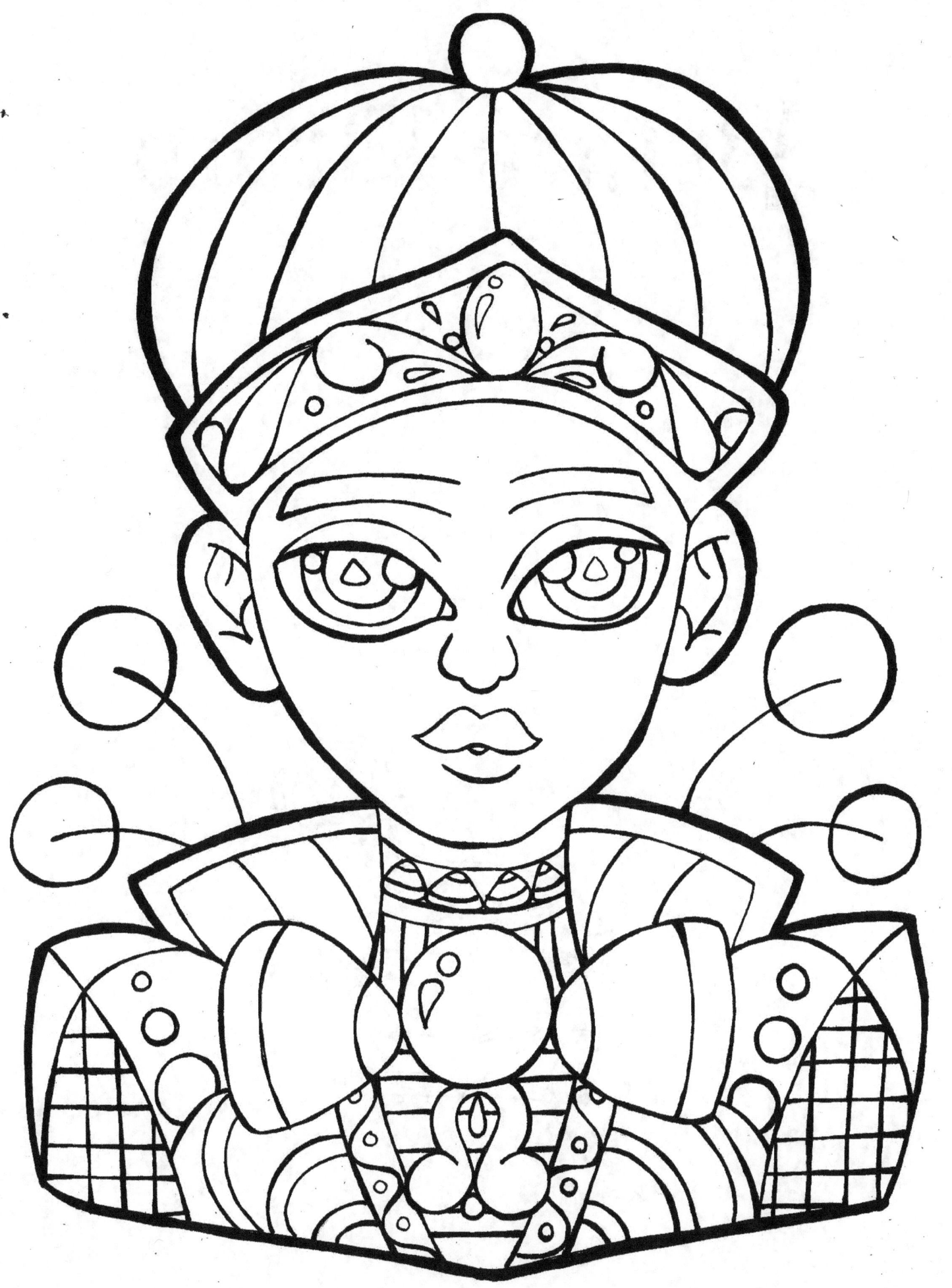

Prince Draco

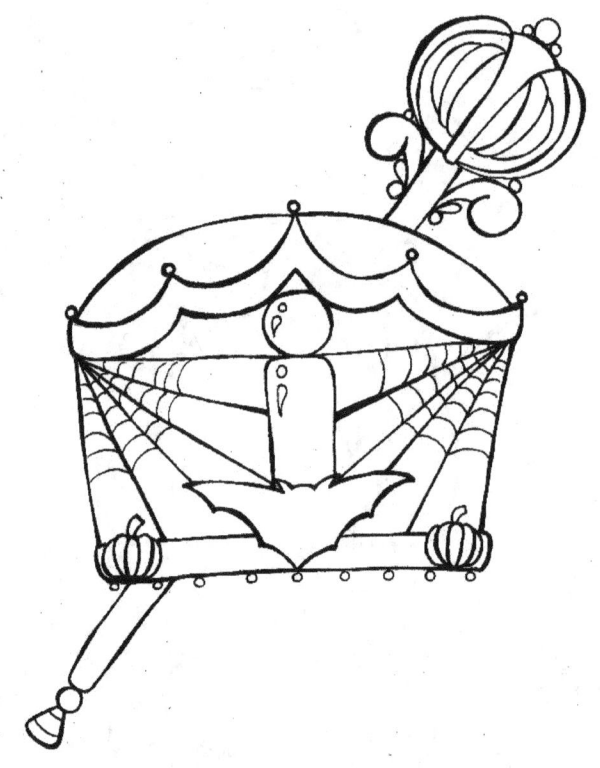

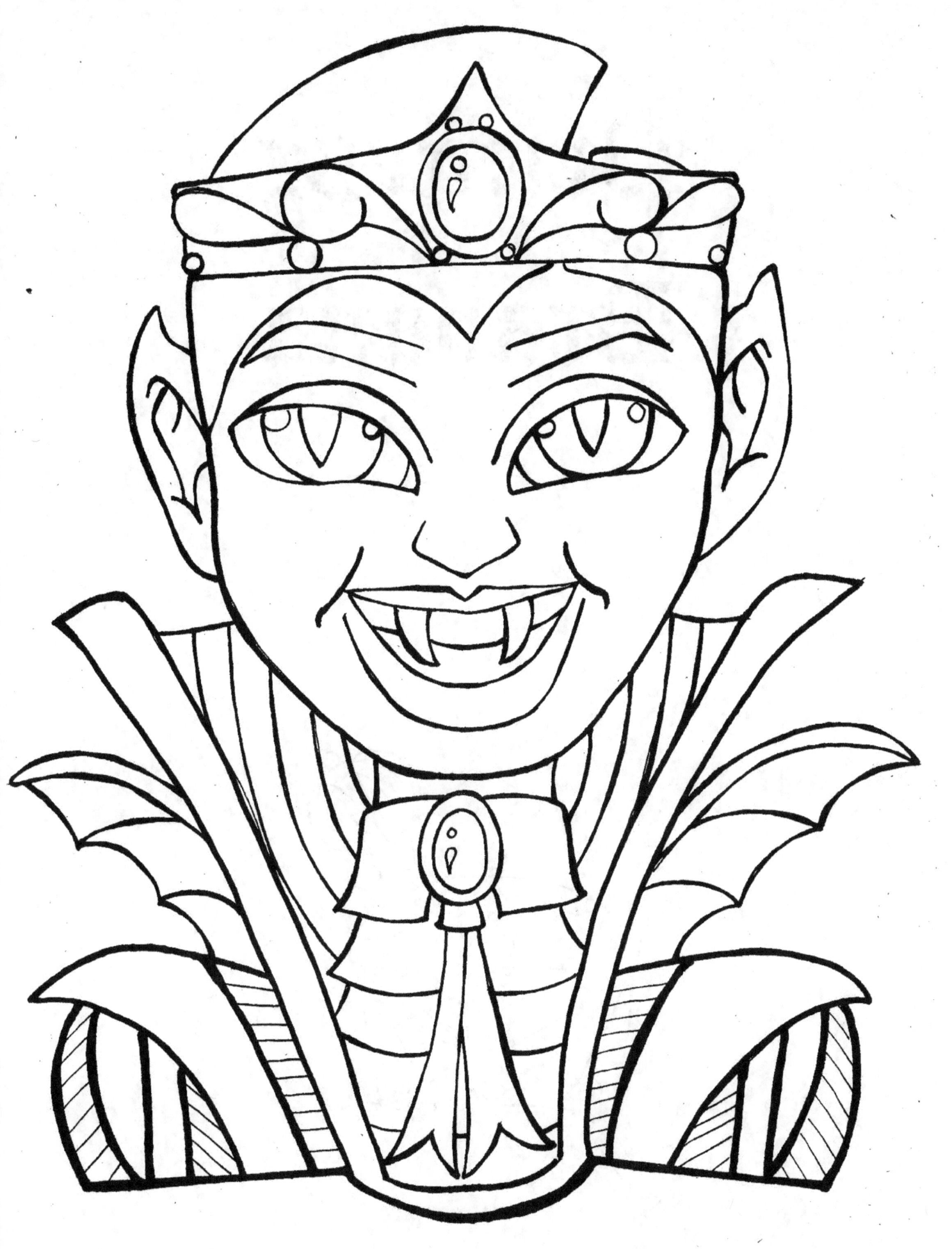

Princess Dravana

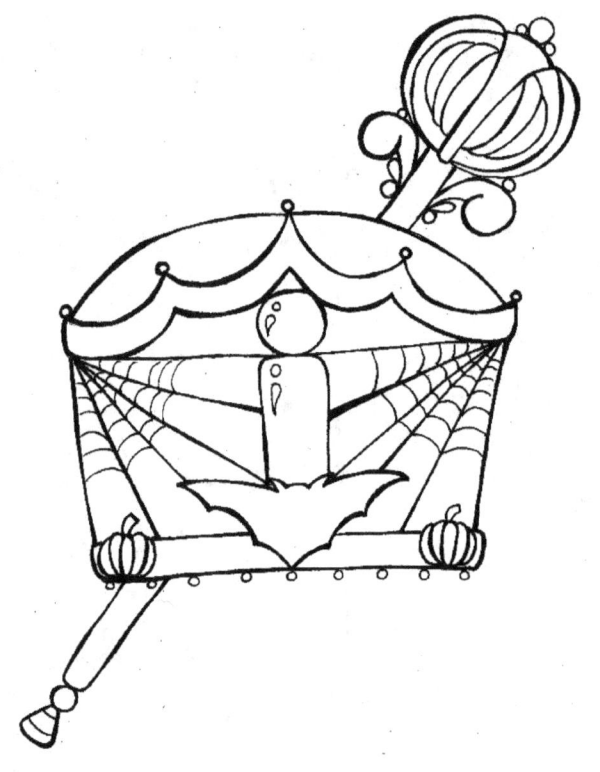

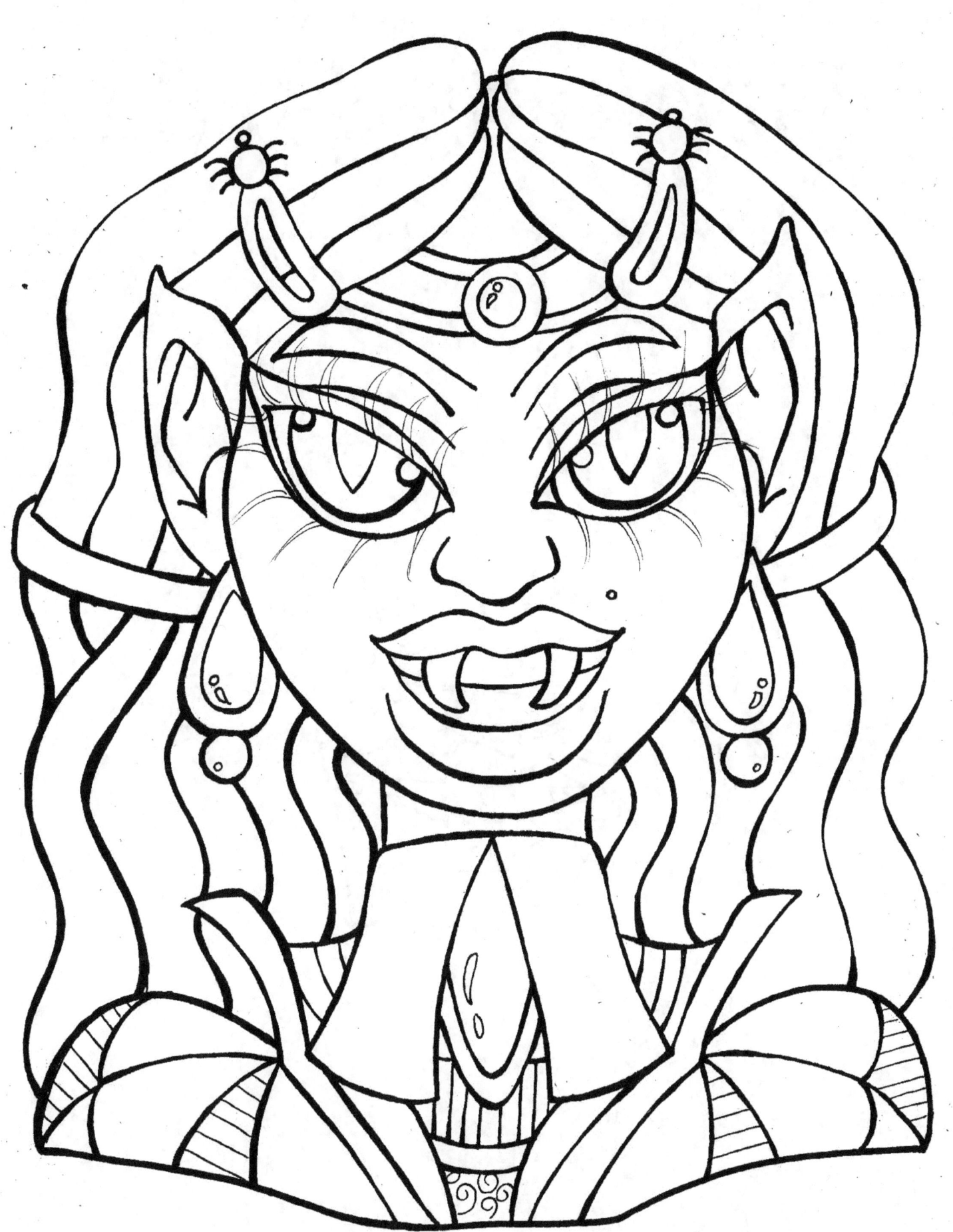

Princess Pella

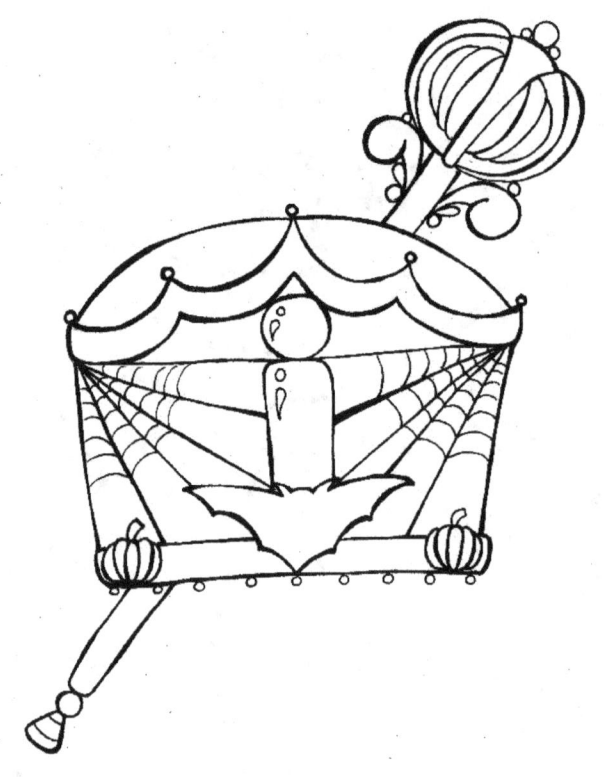

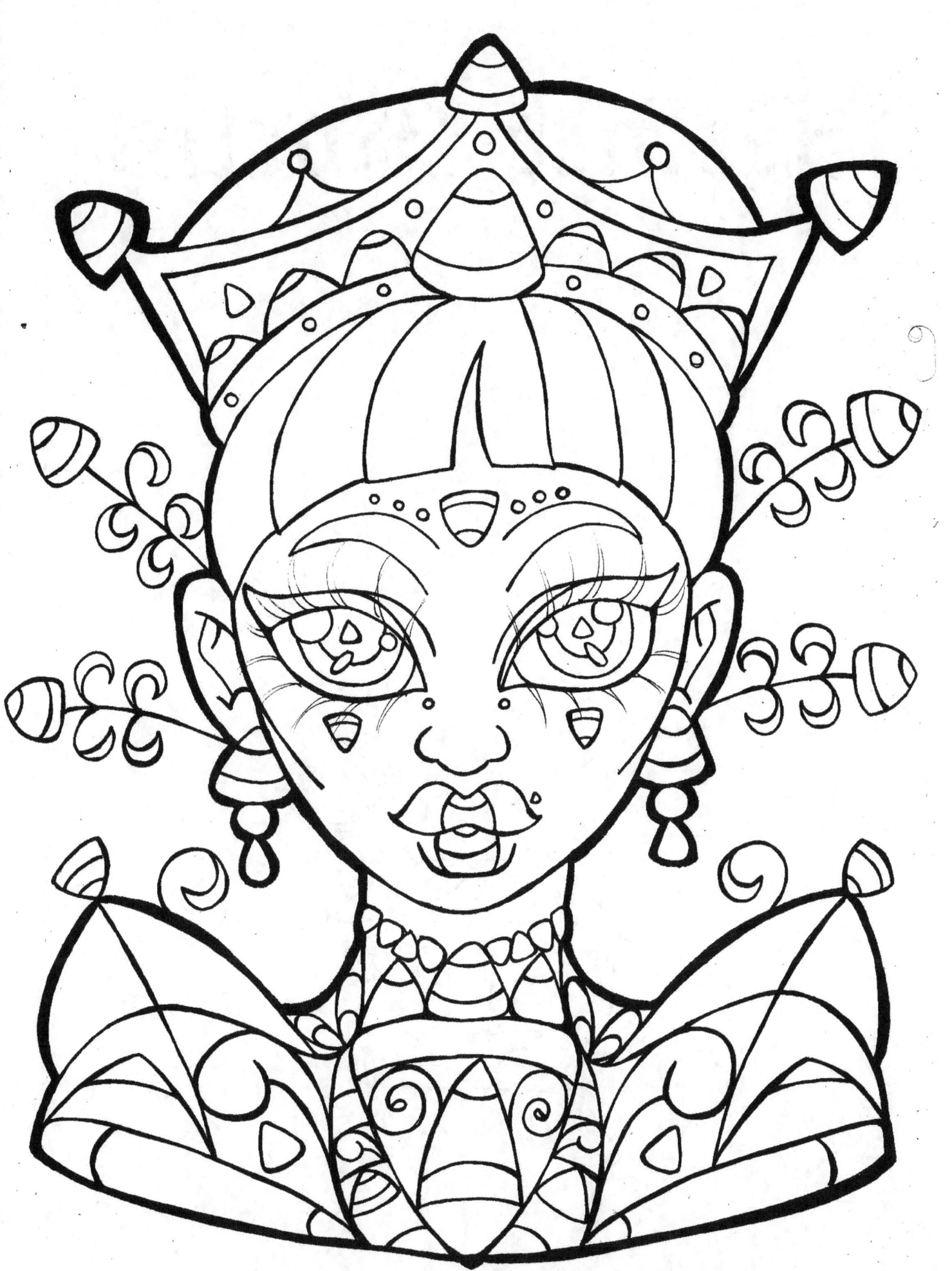

Prince Mortis

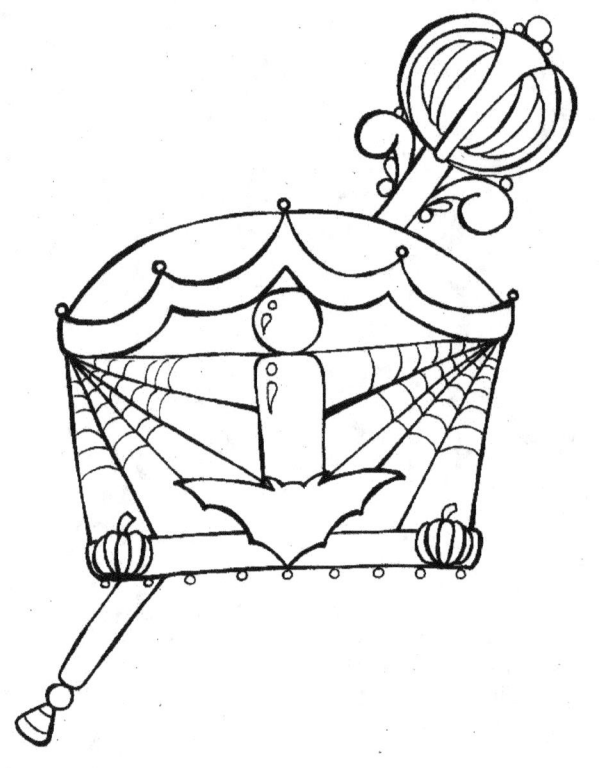

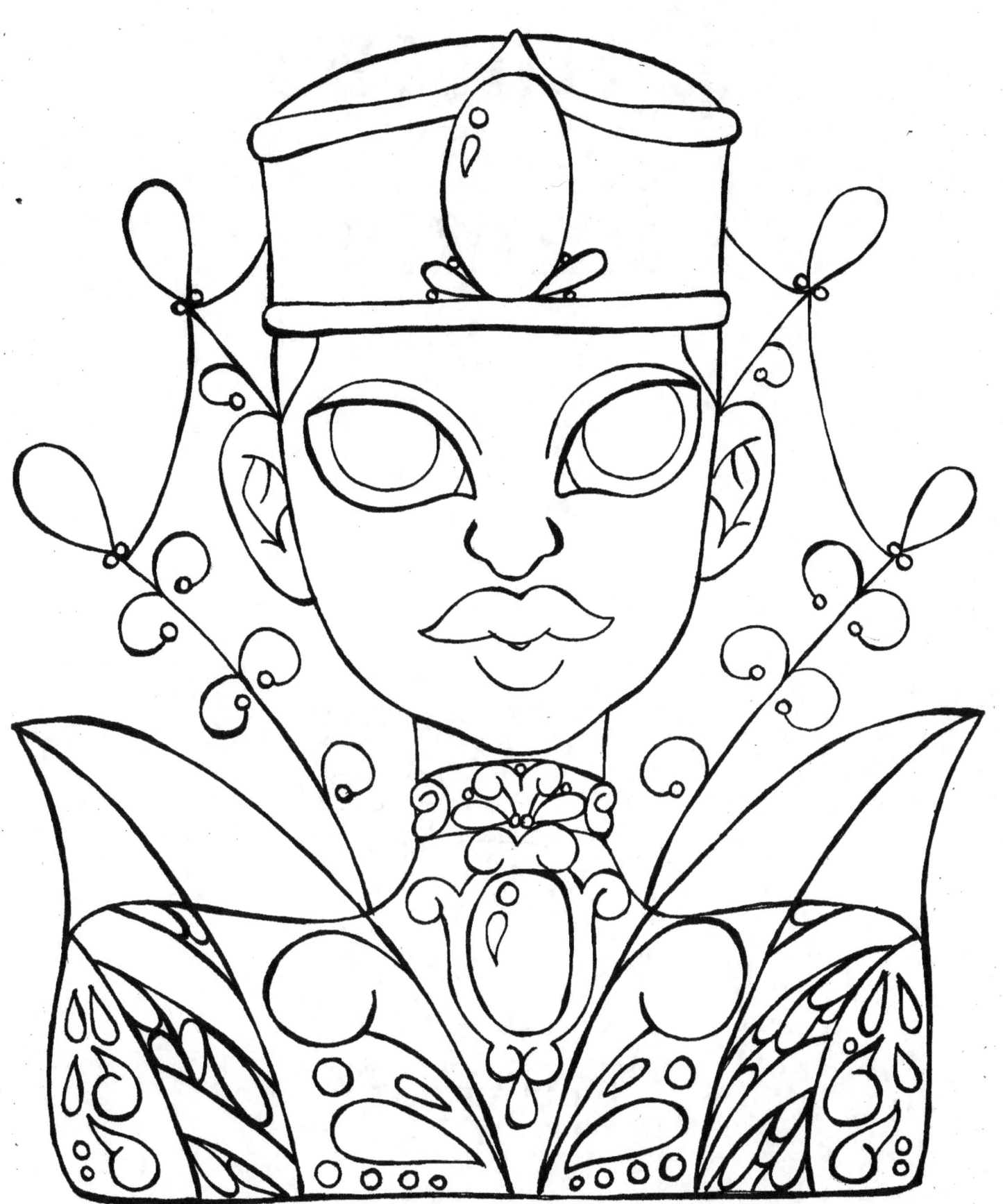

Princess Lamia

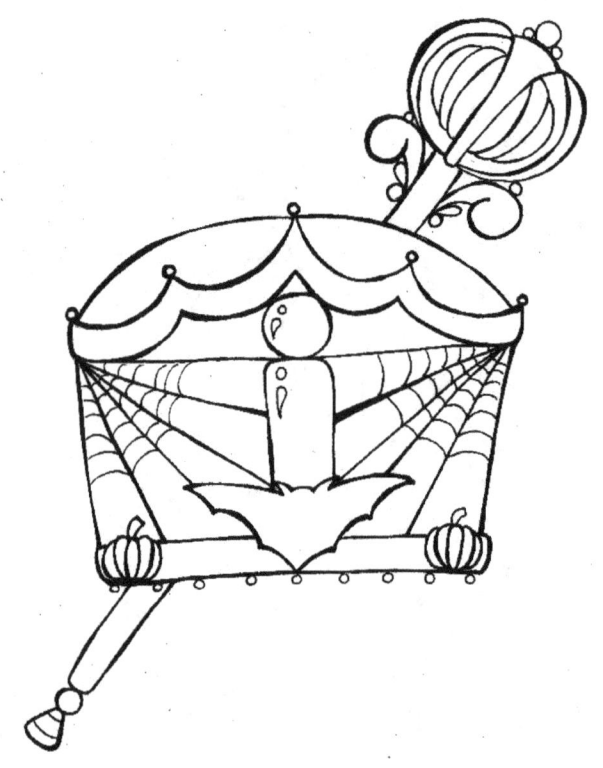

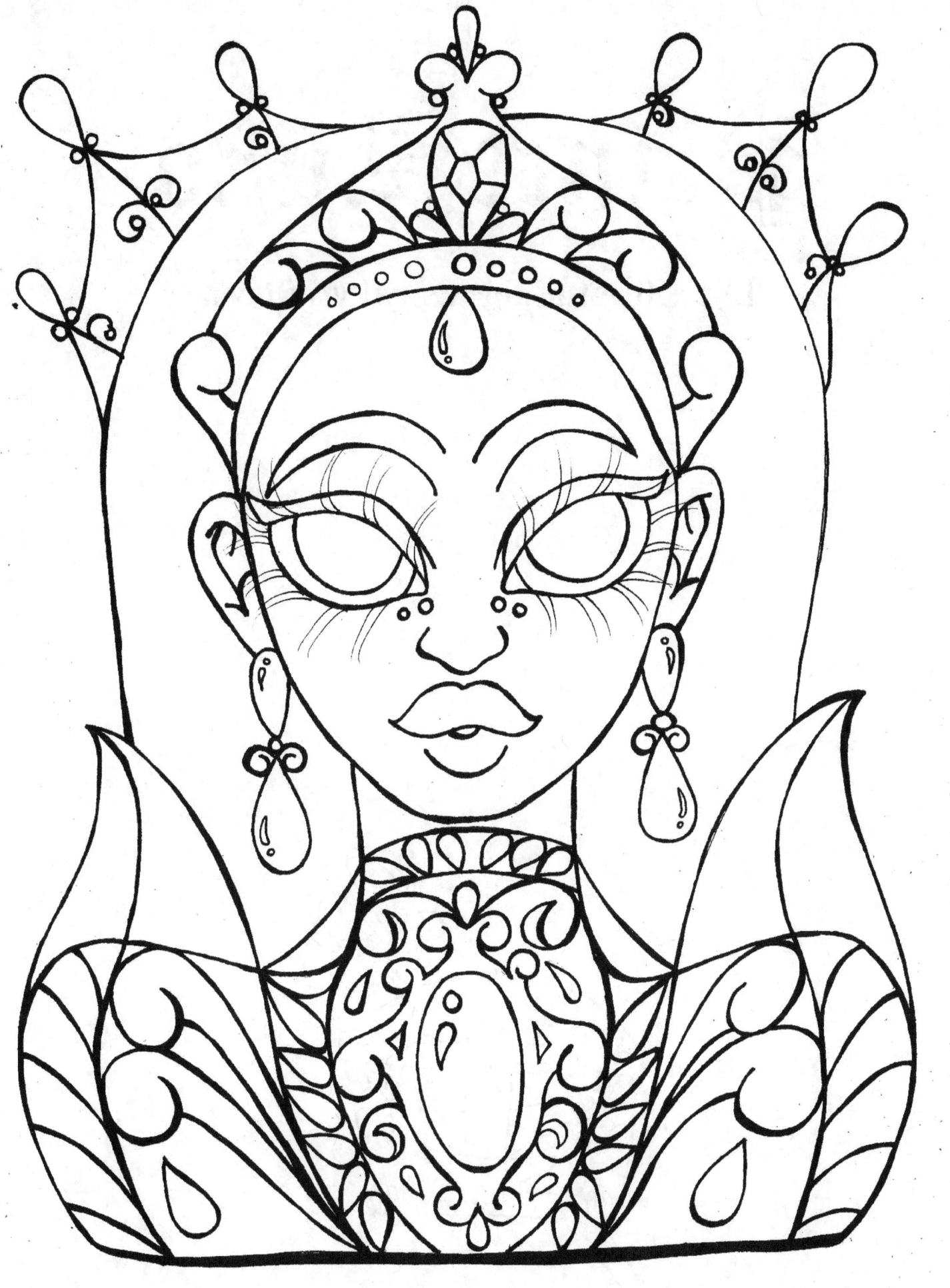

Prince Luko

The Eldest of the Royal Children

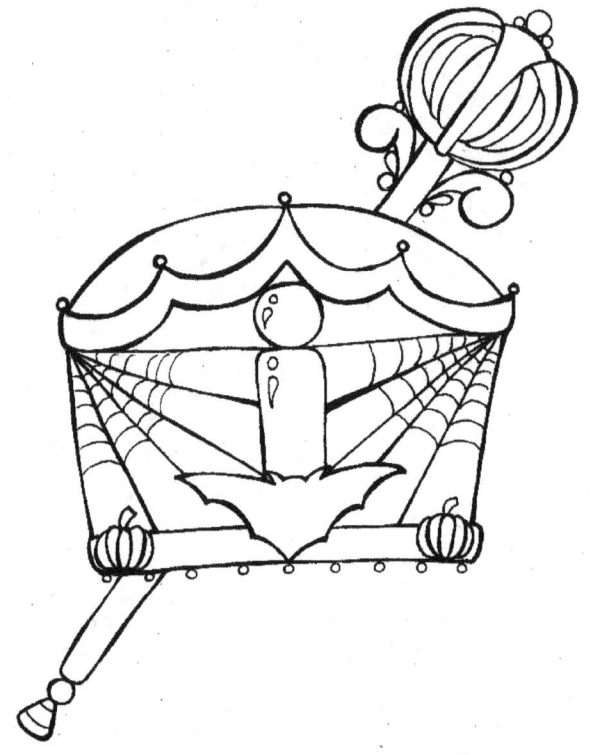

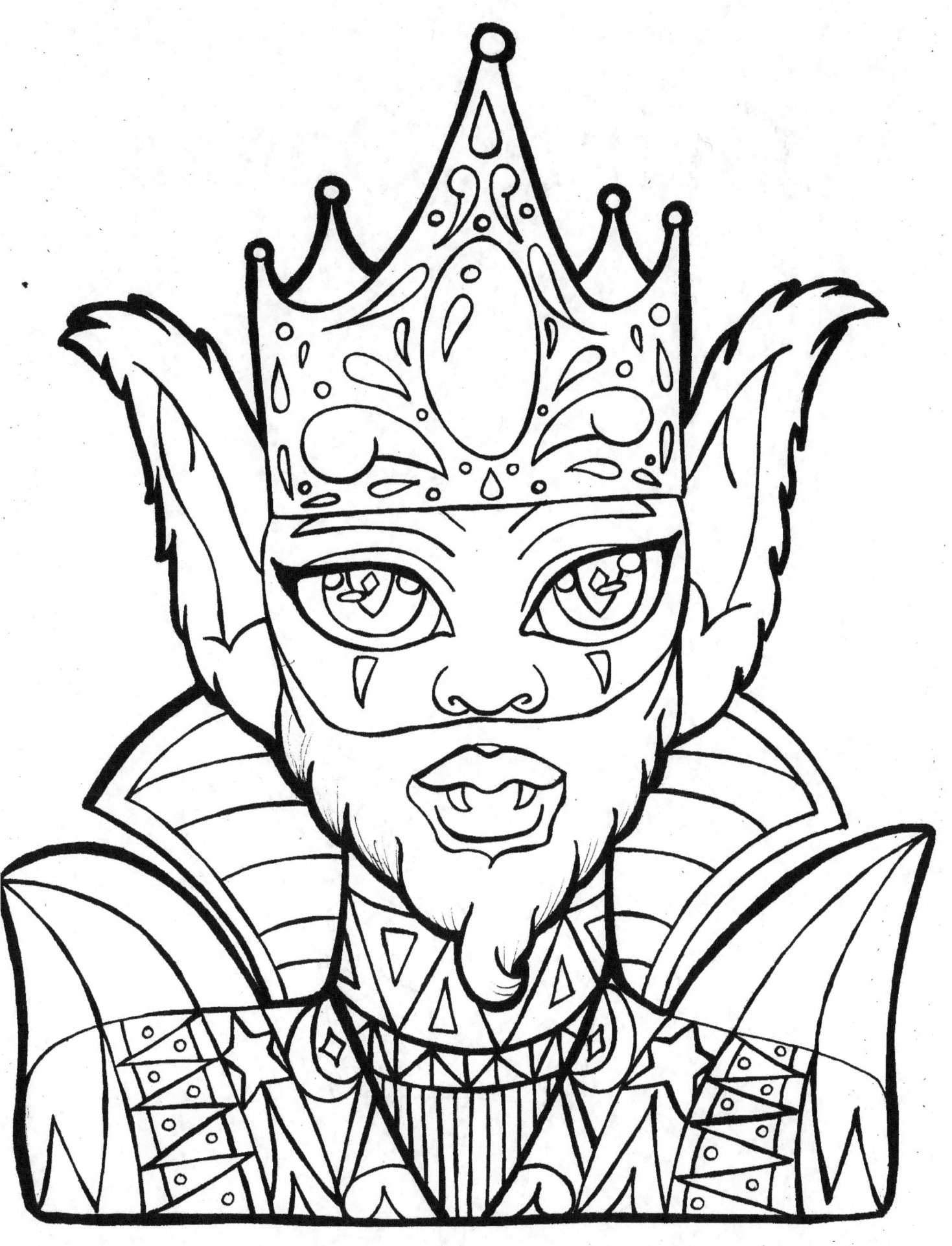

Prince Hoseo

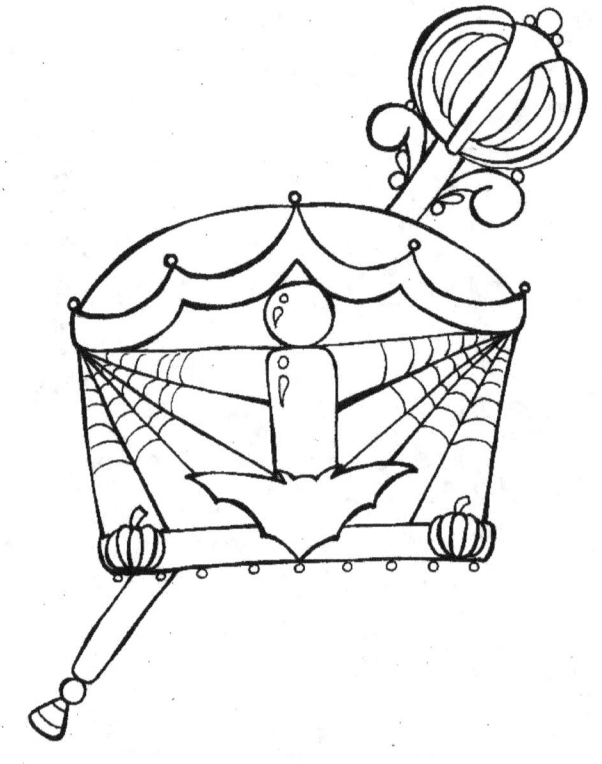

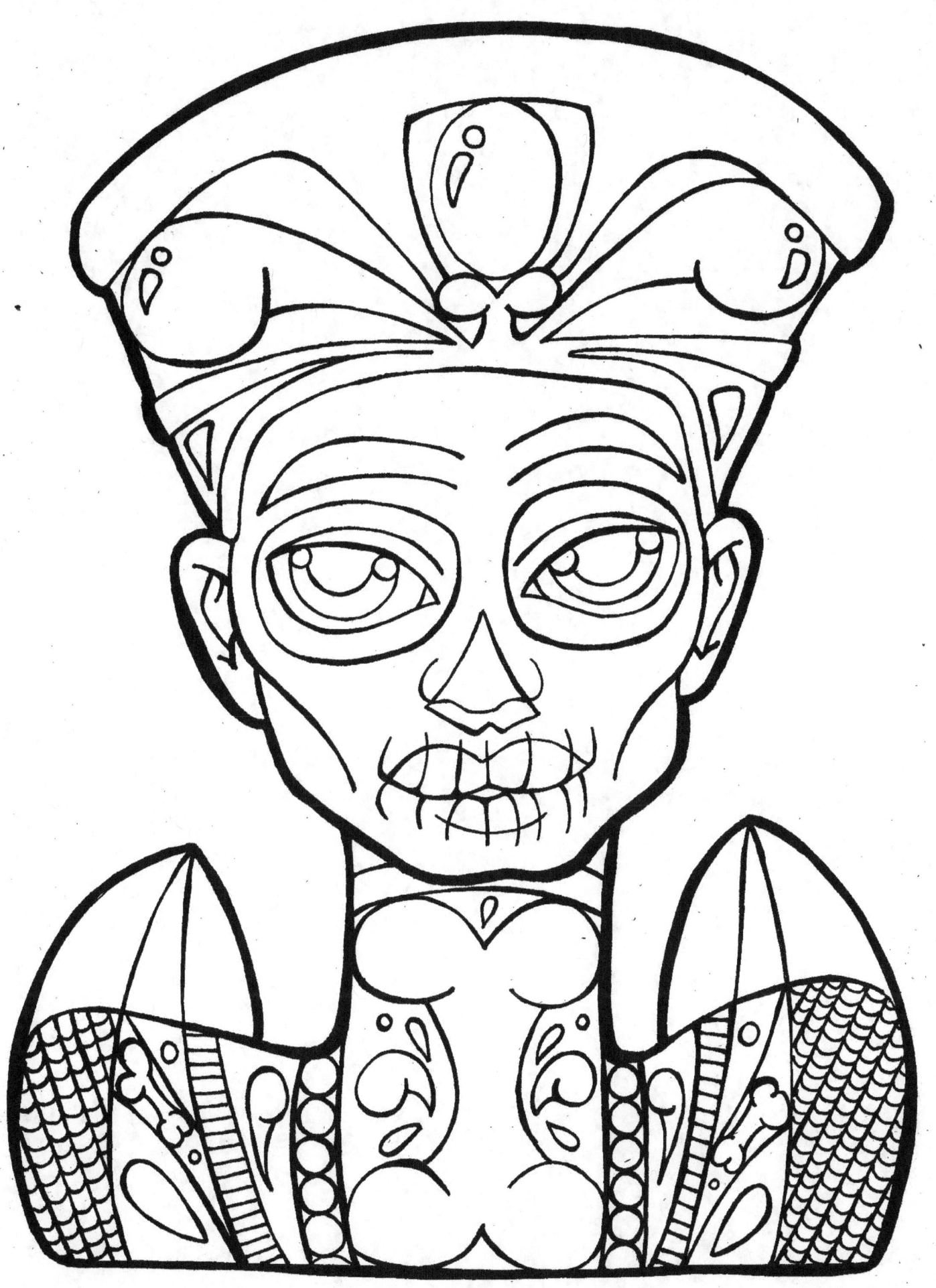

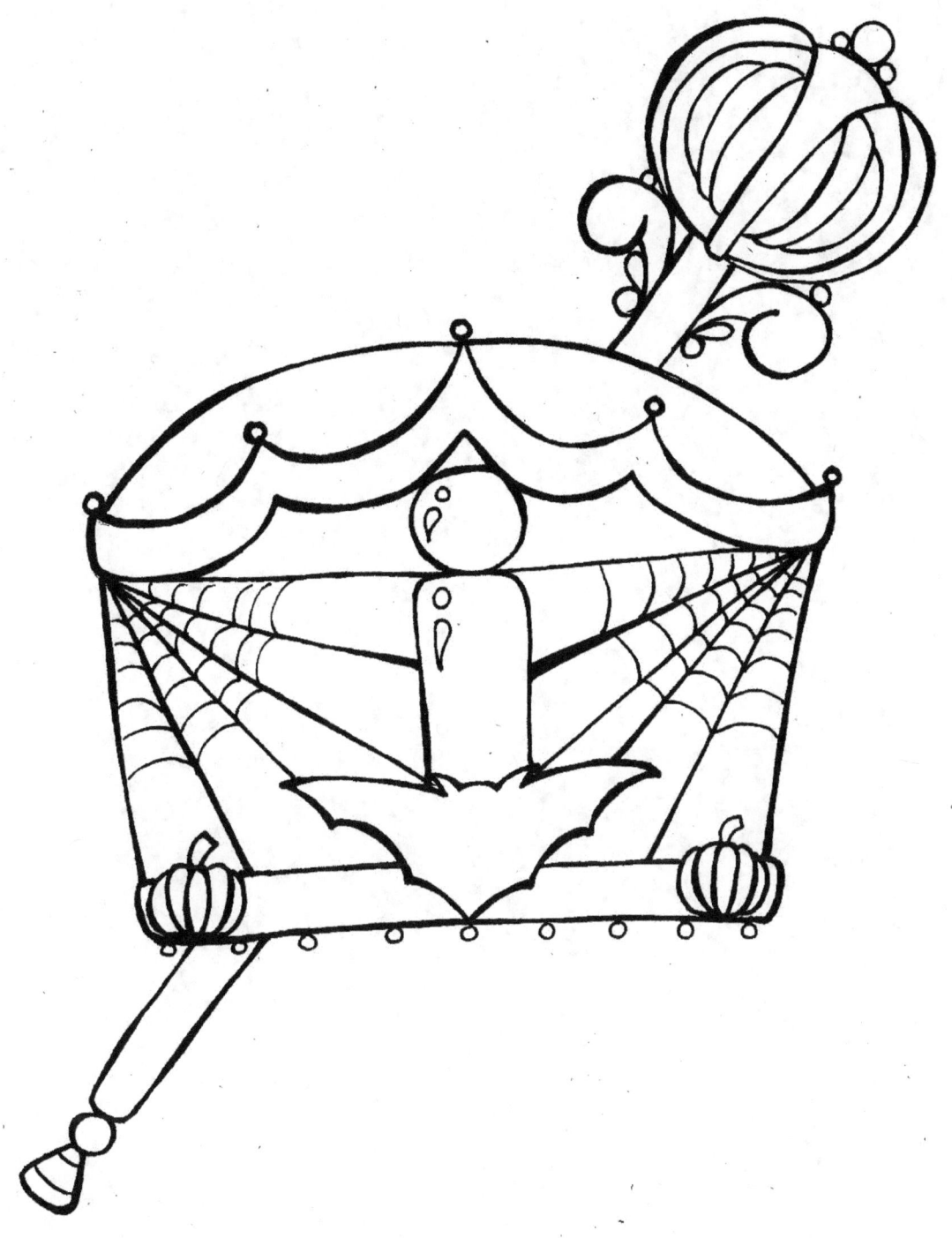

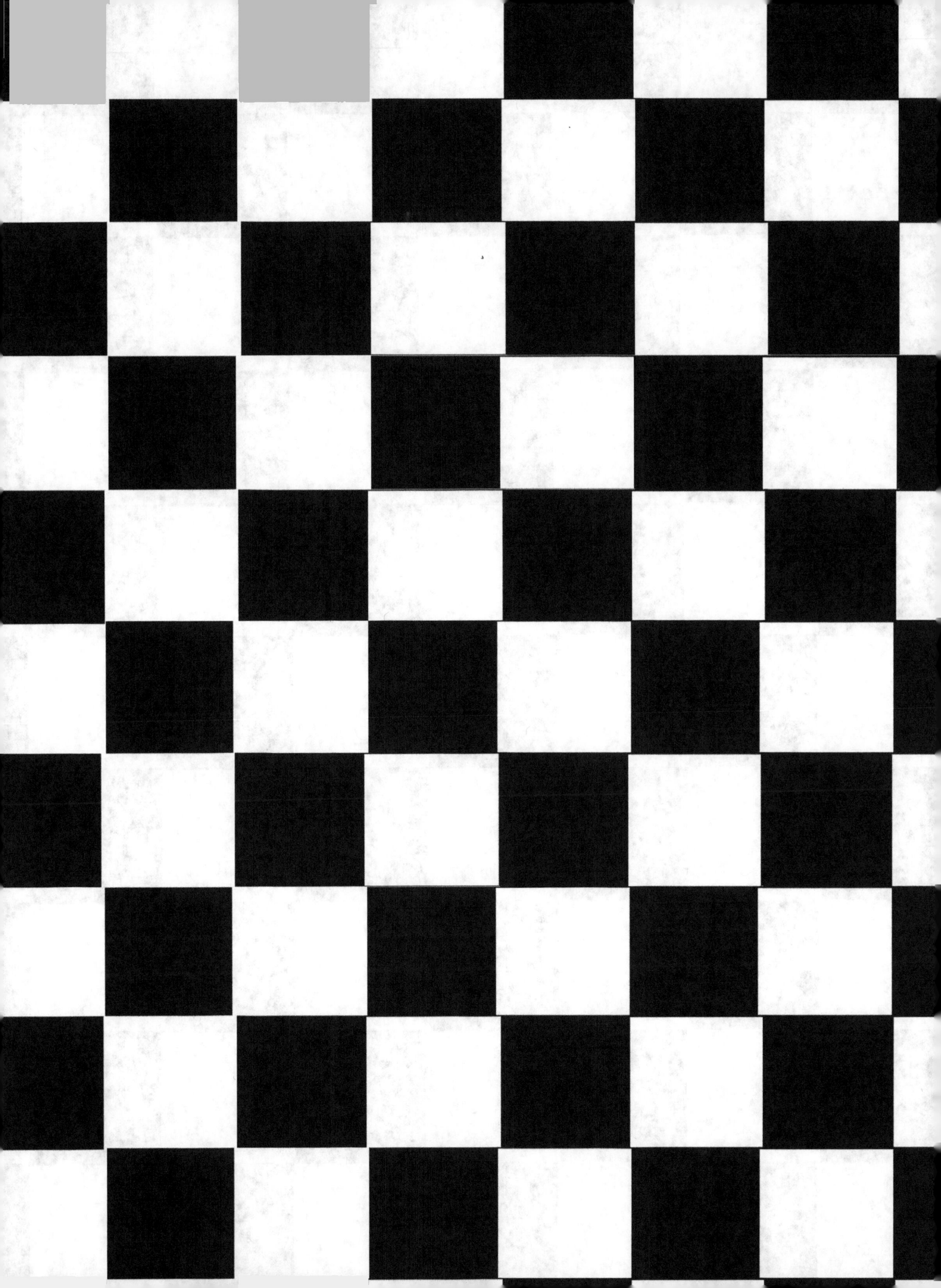

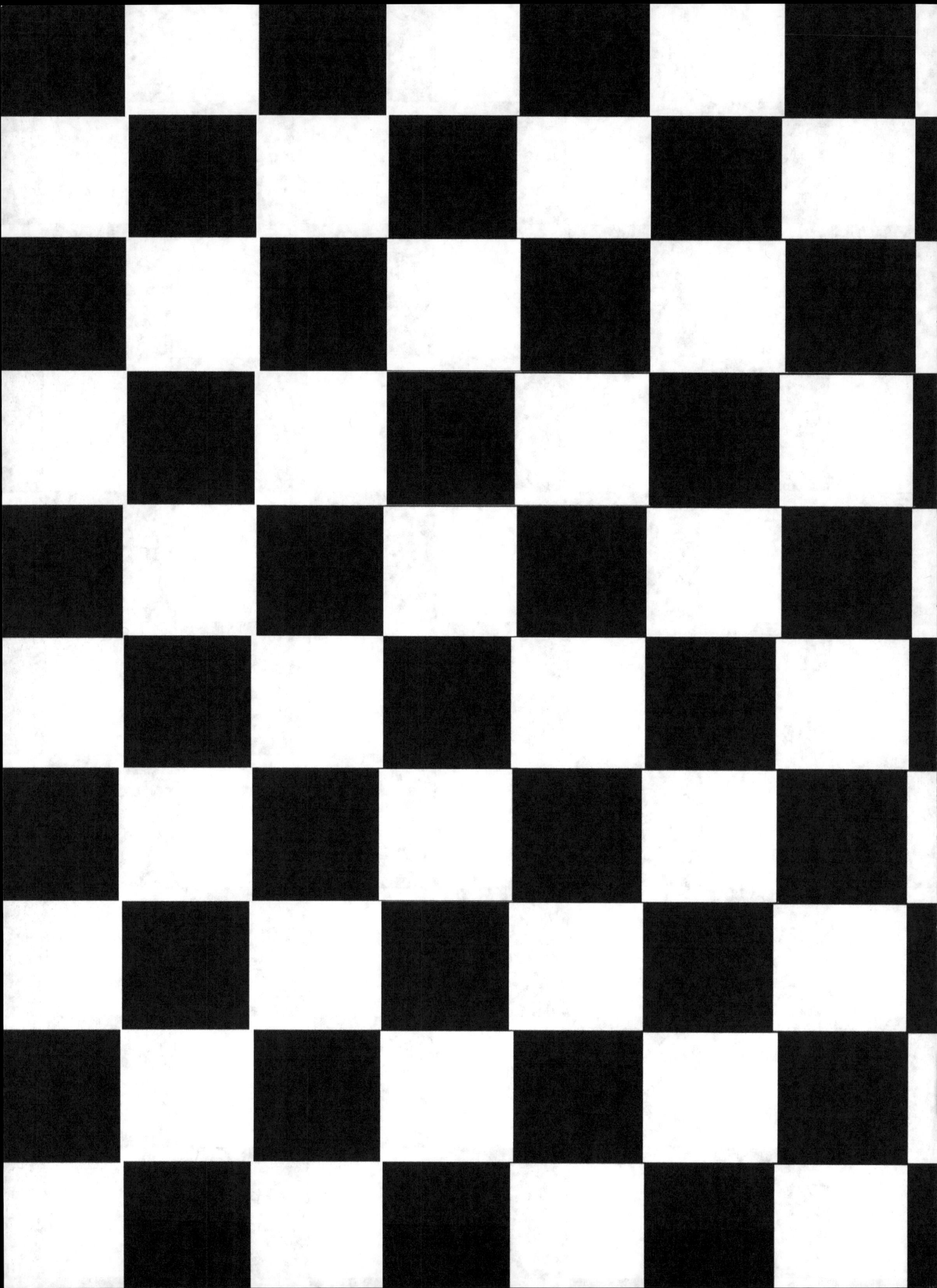

To be continued...........

www.ingramcontent.com/pod-product-compliance
Lightning Source LLC
Chambersburg PA
CBHW062343220526
45469CB00008B/2825